To Dale, S
And
Zoey

LIFE'S ADVENTURES
FROM THEN TILL WHEN

A Compilation of True Life's Adventures
New Songs and Songs My Friends Wish I Would Record

Bill Tripp

ACKNOWLEDGEMENTS

I wish to acknowledge and thank Kay Palmer for her help
and support in creating this book.

TABLE OF CONTENTS

LIFE'S ADVENTURES

OFFIE

Offie was my Great Uncle Ledrew's brother. Offie found him a woman that he really fell for and he decided to get married. They set up housekeeping in a cabin that Uncle Ledrew had on one of his farms. They made arrangements with him to farm the place and pay for it when he sold his crop in the fall. Part of this deal included what Ledrew called the "slow mule," because he was. The farmers would order their supplies from New Bern, NC. A paddle wheel riverboat would deliver them at a designated time to a dock on the Neuse River, near Fort Barnwell.

Offie had plowed all his fields and they were ready to plant. He was supposed to meet the boat that morning. He got up before daylight and since it was still cold in the mornings, he went out to get some kindling and started a fire in the wood cook stove and the wood heater. He had woken his wife up when he first went out and told her to fix some breakfast and a lunch for him to take with him. When he came back in, she was still in the bed. He again woke her up and repeated his request. He then went back out to harness the mule and wagon for the trip. He came back inside again and found her still asleep. With this, he found a pen and paper and left a note. "Sleep on sleeping beauty. Offie's gone."

Uncle Ledrew said Offie brought the mule and wagon back to him and apologized. He said he wouldn't be needing them after all. He told him the land was ready to plant and maybe he could plant it and get some benefit out of it. With that, Offie left and was not heard from for over twenty years.

When Offie reappeared, he revealed that he had gone to Walterboro, SC and farmed with some relatives - Marvin Tripp, Uncle Ledrew's son, Jim Trippe, one of Ledrew's brothers, and Jim's son James Ashley Trippe.

Yes, he spelled his last name differently from us.

Offie's bride never remarried and they never divorced or ever lived together again. They lived in the same general area for the rest of their lives.

FISHING AND HUNTING

Barnwell State Park was about five miles from my house and was about the only place to go during the summer when we were out of school. There were picnicking and swimming areas, but no fishing.

There was what we called a float, although it didn't float. It was a concrete slab on pilings about four inches above the water. The sides were all closed in with lattice strips so you couldn't go underneath it. We played games where we would hide from whoever was "it." I had found a place where the lattice molding was missing at the bottom corner just enough so that I could slip through. I could go up underneath the float and there was enough room to breathe. You could hide as long as you wanted to.

While I was hiding one day, the bream were biting my nipples and a little black mole I had on my side.

I got the idea that if they wanted to bite that bad maybe I could catch some of them. The next day I brought a snuff can filled with fishing worms and about sixteen inches of cat gut fishing line with a hook on the end.

When I went to the float, I took my beach towel and a cloth bag with me. I went underneath the float and started fishing. They would bite as fast as I could bait the hook. I got my bag full of big bream and wrapped them in my beach towel.

There was a concession stand where you could buy hamburgers, hot dogs and other snacks. Food was sold out of one end of building but at the other end of the same room, there was a guy that would give you a wire basket that you could put your clothes or other personal items in. He would put your numbered basket in a numbered slot in the back. When you wanted it, you gave him your number and he would get it for you. I had gotten a basket and put my towel with the bag of fish wrapped up in it and checked it in. He was paying no attention to who put what in the baskets.

I was standing in the hamburger line and I heard the fishes' tails flapping. I was hoping no one else had heard it. They didn't at first but it persisted and finally he went to investigate what was going on. He came back with the basket and the fish flapping in it. He couldn't remember who the basket belonged to.

When that happened, I left the line and never came back to get my towel or fish.

On another occasion, I was fishing in the little creek that was dammed up to create the swimming lake.

The water went over the spillway then through a holding pond and finally over another spillway at a bridge. I was fishing with a similar rig, only with a longer line. I had no fishing pole or anything that would give away my true activity. There was a sharp left turn in the creek about fifty feet below the bridge. The bank was steep and the water had washed out a deep place where the fish collected. When a car came by, I would hide behind a big tree behind me when I was fishing. Normally I would catch a fish and go hide it under a log or something. On this particular morning, I had brought some crabs to fish with. Bream love crabmeat. I was sitting on the bank and had a long string of fish with a large catfish on the very end of the string. I had the string tied beside me. All of a sudden, the game warden was right behind me. I dropped the string of fish into the water. He had driven past the bridge, parked up the road then slipped back up on me. I pretended to be feeding the fish crabmeat. He immediately started looking behind logs and everywhere else for fish or whatever he was looking for. About this time, my long string of fish slowly floated up to the top of the water and across the creek. Then the catfish started splashing around, flipping his tail and really cutting up.

My heart sank, I knew I was caught, but the game warden was so busy looking elsewhere he didn't see it. The long string of fish slowly floated back underneath the water. When he tired of looking, he came back and told me I'd have to leave because I was not supposed to be in that area. I left and went home but I kept thinking about those fish. About ten o'clock that night I got on my bicycle and rode it to the park. It was a pitch-black night. Every so often lighting would light up the area and I could see where I was going and move up a little.

The gate to the park was closed but I could slide my bicycle underneath it with room to spare. The only problem was the park ranger's house was right inside the gate and he had some dogs. I surely didn't need them to start barking at me. I pushed my bicycle quietly past the house. The wind that was blowing from the approaching storm helped some. I continued down the road to the bridge. I left my bicycle just off the road and walked towards the place where I had left my string of fish tied. I would take a few steps each time the lighting would light up the area. I finally made it and found my string of fish and took them back to my bicycle. I used the same tactics to get back to the highway. I made it home about thirty minutes later. I dressed the fish and the family enjoyed a fried fish dinner the next day. They never knew all that I went through to provide it.

Sometimes before church on Sunday morning, I would slip into the back of the parkland and hunt squirrels. For this venture, I didn't need to go in the gate. There was a fire line that I would follow into the park. I used a single shot twenty-two rifle with short bullets. It didn't make much noise. I could kill four or five squirrels and be back home by eight, plenty of time to get ready to go to church. This reminds me of a squirrel hunting trip I had when I was living on the river near Ft. White, Florida. Hunting in this area was totally different. Every tree had something for a squirrel to eat. They would raise three litters a year. This made for many squirrels to hunt. The live oaks and Spanish moss made a shotgun the better choice. Tommy Tatum, a friend of mine, wanted to come down and go hunting with me. Tommy was from Tennessee and was used to hunting squirrels with a twenty-two. I told him he should bring his shotgun but he assured me his rifle would be all he needed.

The first day he got there, we didn't have much time to hunt. It was afternoon and we only got in a couple of hours. I killed a few more squirrels than he did and he changed his mind about using the shotgun. The next morning we drove my old Dodge pickup to a place I was sure the squirrels would be plentiful. It was a foggy morning and we got to the place about daylight. The trees were shaking and squirrels were running everywhere.

We both jumped out and started shooting squirrels. I came back to the truck after a few moments and put some squirrels in that I had killed. I told Tommy we would meet back at the truck at about eleven o'clock. I got some more shotgun shells and started off down a little road. We both were shooting regularly, but we eventually got out of hearing range. We each killed lots of squirrels and arrived back at the truck at eleven o'clock for a sandwich. I had forty-five squirrels and Tommy had forty-eight. He really started rubbing it in. He had beaten me, the reputed champion squirrel hunter at my own game.

We sat and ate our sandwiches and he continued to gloat. When we finished eating, we got in the truck and I drove down the road that I had been hunting on. After about three miles, I pulled off the road got out and told him I'd be right back. I had killed so many squirrels I couldn't carry them all. I had found an old five-gallon bucket and filled it. I had left it in the woods behind a tree. When I brought it back to the truck, poor Tommy wilted. It contained another thirty or forty squirrels. His championship status was short lived.

When I lived In Three Rivers near Ft. White, Florida I used to go hunting a lot by myself. My place was in the extreme corner of Suwannee County. Across the river in Gilchrist County was a big uninhabited tract of land. If you went straight through, it was about three miles deep to a road. However if you went parallel to the river, you could go twenty miles before you hit a road. I used to paddle an inflatable life raft across the river, and hide it in the woods and hunt the area. I would get a few squirrels and come back home. This one particular day I went over and hunted, and got my ten or so squirrels. When I decided to come home, a thick fog rolled in on me and I didn't know which way to go. I usually carried a compass but this time I didn't. I sat down with my back up against a large oak tree. It was getting dark. When it got dark, you couldn't see your hand in front of your face. I was thinking I'd just have to sleep here until daylight. Then I heard a big cat scream. It sounded like it was right behind me. It scared me fully awake! I knew I would not sleep. Panthers were in this area and I wouldn't be able to see him if he licked my nose. I was sure he could smell my squirrels and might want them. The night was very quiet and his squall had raised goose bumps all over my arms.

After what seemed like an hour, I heard the rumble of a distant train. I could hear it for a long time. I knew the only railroad was on the other side of the river and ran along highway twenty-seven from Ft. White to Branford. I got my bearings and started walking in that direction. I held out one hand so I wouldn't run into anything. I continued this until I got to the river. I couldn't see anything until I reached the river. Then my feet splashed in the water.

I didn't know whether to go up river or down to my raft. The outside light was always left on until I got home. Not this night though, it was pitch-black. All I could do was feel my way along the edge of the water. I had passed the cabin by at least three hundred yards. By the time I realized it, I had to return to about where I had hidden my raft. I found the raft after searching a few moments and paddled home across the river.

There was one little night light on inside that was not visible until you were very near. It must have been five o'clock by the time I made it home. A night I'll never forget!

ME AND COUSIN R.V.

I had a cousin R.V. McDowell, my mother's sister's boy. R.V. was about my same age and when we went to visit, I enjoyed spending time with him. They really lived in the sticks. Everything was very basic, no indoor plumbing and a wood heater to heat one room. When you're 14 years old, none of that matters. The area was called Hell's Neck because people said there was one way in and no way out.

One summer I went to stay with them and work in the tobacco fields. We would get up before daylight and take a mule and a wagon to the tobacco barn. The field where we worked that day would be nearby. The mule would pull a tobacco drag that was 6' x 4' x 4' down a row and we would crop the bottom three or four leaves of ripe from the tobacco plant. We would talk to the mule and he knew to keep up with us and did a great job. When we had filled the drag, we would take it to the barn where there were other helpers stringing tobacco on sticks.

On this one particular day, we were working at the far end of the field and it started to rain. Everybody ran to the barn. They asked me to bring the mule. I disconnected the single tree and climbed up on his back. I was holding the single tree, pulled up the trace chains and held them in front of me. I was riding back to the barn down this little sandy road and there was a big ditch on the right side of the road. All of a sudden, a big clap of thunder and lightning caused the mule to bolt. The single tree slipped down about three feet and started hitting the mule every time he would jump. Then he really went wild! He and I parted ways when he was about halfway across that ditch and I fell into the bottom of it. There was nothing to slow my fall but briars. If you don't count the scratches, the worst thing that was hurt was my pride. Just to think I had let a mule throw me!

After each drag, we would climb up in the barn and hang the tobacco on the tiers. When the barn was full, then the curing process began. This was an old wood-fired barn and would have to be watched around the clock. We would have to check the thermometer and adjust the draft on the wood heater to keep the temperature right.

It was cold at night so we had built a fire to keep warm. R.V. said that he was hungry and we both agreed that it would be nice to have a snack. Way off in the distance you could hear a rooster crowing. R.V. said that it was coming from a place he called Aunt Cossy's. He said he was going to get us something and would be back in a little while.

When he returned an hour or so later, he had a chicken, rice and some seasoning. We found a cast iron pot that was already at the barn. He dressed the chicken and put it in the pot. After it cooked a while, we added the rice and other things. Maybe it was because we were hungry and cold, but that chicken and rice was the best I have ever eaten. I still think about it now and then. To this day, one of my favorite things to cook is chicken and rice.

JOE SKEETER

Joe Skeeter was an old timer that I knew when I lived in Three Rivers near Fort White, Florida. Joe was known to do a little illegal fishing from time to time. After all, he had been doing it since before it was illegal. His passion at the time was to fish with dynamite. On this particular day, someone had reported his activity to the game warden. This time of year the big roe mullet would swim from the Gulf of Mexico up the Suwannee River, the Santa Fe River and finally to the Ichetucknee River. The Ichetucknee was crystal-clear and when a big school of mullet came by, he would throw the dynamite and reap a bounty of fish.

The game wardens had slipped in and hid early in the morning and was waiting on him. When he lit the fuse for the first time, they stood up pointing their guns at him. This startled him so that he dropped the dynamite in the boat. Realizing what he had done he jumped from the boat just in time. His boat was blown to smithereens. The game wardens caught him. He lost his boat, his motor, his fishing equipment, fish, and was taken to jail all in one day. Not a good day for Joe.

WHY I DON'T BUY A LICENSE

The same Joe Skeeter, that I told you about fishing illegally, also liked to take the kids fishing. He had a favorite spot where they could fish from the bank and catch little bream. It was also the place where he tied up his boat. His little wooden boat was pulled more than half way out of the water, chained and pad locked to a large cypress tree. Joe was not up to standing and fishing with the kids, so he sat down in the boat and fished from there. The game wardens had gotten sneaky and didn't wear their uniforms. They would come up the river paddling a canoe and paddle right up to you to check you out. This particular morning they came up and checked Joe out. They asked him where his life jacket or flotation device was, since it was required by law when you were fishing from a boat. They wrote him a citation. I didn't think this was at all reasonable since he was half way on the shore. (See photos of boats from this era.)

Not too long after this event, I was scuba diving in the Santa Fe River. It was unusually clear because it had not rained for a while and the water was low. I found an old spear gun that had green moss growing all over it. You could tell this thing had been in the water for years. I had been diving with Larry Johnson on this day and Larry ran out of air before we made it back to the cabin. We were exiting the river at the boat landing and Larry yells, "What did you do with the spear gun?" I told him I left it out in the river. His ears were full of water and he didn't hear me so he yells a second time, "What did you do with the spear gun?" Now we had the attention of everyone at the boat landing.

We took our tanks off at the landing and I told Larry to wait with the tanks while I got the car because the tanks were much too heavy to carry that far. When I came back, the game warden had gone out in a little boat and fished the spear gun out of the river. He asked if it belonged to me. I said, "I guess it does. I found it in the river." He said spear guns were illegal and he wrote me a ticket. This didn't set well with me either, so I decided that I would never again buy a license. When I decided this, I was in very good physical shape and I was pretty sure I could out run and out swim the game wardens.

A year or so after this, my dad's friend Toby from North Carolina wanted to come visit me. Dad knew that he liked to fish and he wanted me to show him a good time. The afternoon before he arrived, I went up to Jameson Run, a little stream that was about a quarter of a mile long, twenty-five yards wide and five feet deep. The mullet were so thick in there it looked like you could walk on them. I decided take Toby to catch some of those mullet the next afternoon.

There was only one two-rut road running to the stream. It split off and the other road went around the spring where the run originated. The bank of the run was high on that side, maybe six or eight feet. You could walk through the woods and see the run but you couldn't get in from that side. Toby and I had gone down to the run. We had a gill net, number three washtub, corn sack and we were catching fish. I might mention here that gill nets were illegal. We were on the high bank side of the run and out of the corner of my eye, I caught a smoky the bear type hat of the game warden peeking over at us. Shortly after that, I heard him start his car and take off to block the road that we would have to use to get out. I yelled to my son Craig who had come with us to take the car and go home. Craig was not old enough to drive legally but knew how. He would be gone before the game warden could block the road. I took our tub, net and fish, and sank them just out of the mouth of the run.

By this time, it was getting dark and Toby and I started swimming down the river. The river ran in the right direction to take us all the way home. It had really gotten dark and Toby was making a lot of noise and splashing. I told him to swim quieter because there were alligators in the river and we didn't want to attract them. Some time later Toby said he was tired and wanted to rest. I told him we would stop and to hold on to the next cypress limb that was hanging over the river, but to let me make sure they're no water moccasins hanging on it first.

We continued on down to my cabin and got out about ten o'clock that night. The next morning I went back before daylight with my boat and motor and got the things we had left in the river. We had a great fish cook out and I thought Toby had a good time. The next year I went to see my Dad in North Carolina and decided to drop by and see Toby. He was having a cook out and musicians were playing on a stage they had set up. He asked me to get my guitar and play a few songs. I got my guitar and he introduced me to his guests. He said, "You people ought to see how this man lives. He scared me to death one night. I want you to know, Tarzan don't have a damn thing on him!"

RABBIT HUNTING

When I was growing up on the farm in Barnwell County South Carolina one of my pursuits was rabbit hunting. Back then, rabbits were everywhere. There was no season on rabbits so you could hunt them any time. We would hunt in the fall and winter. We didn't keep count, but I remember one time I had a number three washtub full of dressed rabbits the next morning. This helped to feed the family.

I had a system worked out with my friend Ken Holcomb; he would drive my car and I would ride shotgun. The local airport, which was almost never used, had two parallel runways. In between these was a tall grassy area that was always loaded with rabbits. We would drive through the grass, which was up to the headlights and the rabbits would run out onto the runways. I could always shoot lots of rabbits.

At other times, we would just drive the back roads at night and shoot rabbits. One foggy night we were driving dirt back roads shooting rabbits and at about two a.m., we came up to a place where some rabbits ran across the road. The rabbits ran off to our right and under an old house. This old house was built about five feet off the ground up on brick columns. It seemed to be abandoned. I got out and went up to the house, looking under it and I saw a rabbit. He ran behind one of the columns about halfway underneath the house. After a little bit, he stuck his head out and I shot him with my double barrel. I went and got him. On the way back to the car to my amazement, lights came on in the house. People were living there. We sped away as fast as we could. Can you imagine the sound of a shotgun going off underneath your bedroom? That would be what I call a rude awaking.

HUNTING WITH LAURIE

Laurie loved to hunt, period. Deer and hogs were his passion. Laurie had a lease on a large tract of land for hog hunting rights. He had hounds for tracking and bulldogs for catching. They were all well trained. The procedure was to release the hounds, and once they bayed the hogs, you would release the catch dogs.

One night Laurie and I were hunting on this tract of land. It had been raining for a week and water was standing in the woods. The graded road that we were on was all that was above water. What we would try to catch were the small ones, which we would put in a box, take them home and feed them. Since it was still drizzling rain any tracks crossing the road would be very fresh. We saw some tracks and Laurie released the hounds. As soon as they got in the woods, they were baying hogs. Laurie yelled for me to release the catch dogs, which I did. So much noise, dogs barking, growling, pigs squealing, water splashing and then Laurie, yelling for me to come and help him.

That very night on the way to meet Laurie, I had bought a new flashlight. This was one of those lights that used a six-volt battery, the kind that has two little coil springs as contacts, one in the middle and one offset. There was a little tab on the bottom at the back of the flashlight that released the battery. The entire bottom would swing open and the battery would come out. When I ran towards Laurie as soon as I got in the fray, I hit something with my flashlight and the battery fell out into the water. There I was down on my knees in the water trying to find my battery. After some time I found it. Then it took a while for me to figure out how to put it back in the flashlight.

I finally got my light on and ran to where Laurie was still calling for help. I ran down a little two-rut road that was also flooded, to a bridge with no side rails that was about one foot above the water. Laurie had a full-grown boar hog by the hind legs and his head under water. There was blood in the water from the dogs that were cut-up pretty bad. They were swimming around the hog. Laurie said "help me pull him out; I don't want to drown him."

I said, "Drown him!" Well I helped him pull him out and we hog-tied him with his feet together, and his tushes (like tusks) tied to his feet. We loaded him up and Laurie picked up the bulldog that was cut the worst and held a handful of mud to his throat where the blood was gushing out. I drove us home with Laurie holding that poor dog in his lap. When we got to Laurie's house, we went down to his hog pin. He had lights down there and I held the light for him while he took a needle and thread, and sewed up the dog's wounds.

After we got the dog taken care of, we took the hog and put him in the hog pen. Laurie managed to untie him and he jumped up ready to fight anybody or anything. After a while, he calmed down. Both the dog and the hog recovered from their ordeal. The hog was fattened up and a year or so later was turned into barbeque.

MOONSHINE

Most people that drank it knew where you could buy moonshine. One of the suppliers that I knew about ran a fish camp on the Savannah River. It was near what was known as Little Hell Boat Landing. Boyed Sanders often said his still was so well hidden that no one could find it. Even flying over it, you could not see anything. Leon Zizzit, a friend and I had gone there to do a little squirrel hunting. We had a small boat with a three HP Elgin outboard motor. So we went down river to a place he had chosen and got on an island formed by the river washing out a new route. This left about a one hundred acre island that was disputed land. Was it in South Carolina or Georgia? Since the river was the state line, it was just neglected. We really didn't care, we just wanted to hunt squirrels.

We started hunting and I had gone about a hundred yards when I came across a well-worn path heading into the interior of the island. I started following the path and after a little while, I hadn't shot any squirrels; but I came across a moonshine still in full operation. There were three men running it. One of them saw me and yelled to the others. They gave me the place, I could hear them hit the river and swim away. I went back to the river the way I had come. There I found Leon had come up to where I had found the path. We were looking around the area and discovered a huge stack of quart jars filled with moonshine packed in boxes. They were covered and well hidden. Then we heard an outboard coming up the river.

THIS BOAT IS SIMULAR TO BOYED'S

Boyed had a twenty-two HP Evinrude. That was about the biggest motor on the river back then. He also had a very big flat bottom boat that could carry quite a load. He passed where we were, turned around and he came in under some limbs hanging over a little cove. Behind the limbs, he could not be seen from the river. He cut the motor off, paddled in the little inlet, got out and tied up the boat. Leon and I had hid behind a big log that was near where he was. We had opened our double barrel shotguns and laid them over the log. We were looking through the barrels at him.

Leon yelled, "Get on the ground face down and don't move." He did and was laying there quivering. We got up and walked over to him, Leon bumped him with the gun barrel and said "now what in the hell would you do if I really was the man?" He got up somewhat relived and said "I couldn't do anything; you had me".

We told him we had spooked his crew and that they had left the still. He gave us each a quart of shine. He told me some time later that it had taken him three months to recover his crew. They had been so afraid to show their faces.

I belonged to a hunting club near Walterboro, S.C. and had planned to hunt with the club on one Saturday morning. Ken Holcomb and Tommy Green, two of my friends, were going with me. At the last moment, Ken told us that he wasn't going because he had a date with a new girlfriend. This had Tommy and me upset. We knew that Ken liked a little moonshine, so we devised a plan. We broke out the quart of moonshine that Boyed had given me and we started giving a little to Ken. Tommy and I kept refilling Ken's glass with shine, while we put water in ours. After drinking a hour or so, Ken was pretty stoned. We all started to Walterboro that afternoon, thinking Ken would sober up by the time we got there.

About midnight we were giving him hot coffee to get him in shape. We were slated to meet at James Ashleigh Trippe's house at four AM. After coffee and breath mints, we thought we had all our bases covered. My great uncle Jim, who was ninety-eight years old, stayed with James, his son. Uncle Jim could not hear unless you yelled at him. We told James and the others gathered there that Ken had gotten sick from eating chocolate covered cherries. Now, he had eaten some of those before the moonshine and had lost them on the way to Walterboro. After a while, everyone left the room except for us and Uncle Jim. He got up and walked over to me and said, "Son, you need to tell that boy to lay off of that moonshine whiskey; that stuff will kill him." I don't think Ken ever managed to explain all this to his new girlfriend. Sorry Ken!

POACHING IN THE KING'S WATERS

My friend and nearest full time neighbor, James, lived up the Ichetucknee River from me. Some days when the weather forecast was good and we wanted to have a fish fry after church, he would call me early in the morning. He would say, "Do you want to go poaching in the king's waters?" I always did. That was the signal for me to get my diving equipment and spear gun and work my way upstream until we met. By this time, we would each have a bag of fish. We would then ice them down and after church, we would dress them and have a fish fry.

Now James was a real pro. He could cook the very best fish and hush puppies you ever ate. After one of our fishing trips during the middle of the week, (I don't recall exactly why we were off but we were) he decided we should have a turtle fry. I didn't think that I would want to eat turtle with so many good fish available. Nonetheless, he was quite adamant, so I started helping him catch turtles. These were what we called streaked head river turtles and they were plentiful. It was no problem to catch all you wanted.

We put turtles in the boat until we had the bottom covered. I had never dressed a turtle, but James had grown up on the river and he was very good at frying just about anything. He dressed them, cut them up in just the right sized pieces and seasoned them just right. We deep-fried the fish and the turtles. The fish were always good, but the turtle was unbelievable. It was delicious and melt in your mouth good. I wound up eating leftover turtle for three days. Mmm . . . so good!

CABIN ROOF

I was spending my vacation working on my cabin. Most of the time I would work a little, fish a little and hunt a little. I always had a few volunteers who would take their vacation at the same time so they could enjoy the hunting and fishing as well. I would provide food, so all that they had to bring was their fishing tackle, their gun and whatever else they wanted. We were working on the flat roof of the cabin, putting new rolled roofing on. The guys asked what we were having for lunch. I said, "I don't know yet."

"What do you mean you don't know yet?"

"I don't know yet." It was getting late in the morning, however so I should start thinking about that. This entire area was very wild back then so I started looking around for a lunch. Before long, a bunch of wild ducks came swimming down the river. I reached over and picked up my old double barrel shot gun, which I had brought up with me and said, "We're having duck!" We were able to eat well all week, mostly fish and squirrels.

My friend Wayne Dunn had a cabin up the river from me and I went up there to help him do some work on his place. His cabin had two stories. The upstairs was open space and we had been putting down a plywood floor over the other wood.

We had brought sleeping bags and were sleeping downstairs. Sometime during the night we were awakened by a weird noise upstairs. It was a growl and it sounded like something was walking across the floor. We got up and I got the shotgun, Wayne got the flashlight and we very cautiously went up the stairs. When we got to the top, we carefully opened the door. The room seemed empty except for a few tools and building material that we had put up there. We stood there looking. All of a sudden, the saw started growling and rolling across the floor. The saw that we had been using had the guard tied open. The trigger was leaking power and it had rolled all over the floor. You could see the saw marks everywhere.

One night when I was living in my cabin, the water was rising rapidly and it would sometimes leave me surrounded by water. This night the water was running through a little cut and marooning me on the island. I could hear all kind of fish jumping in this little cut so I decided to set my gill net across it. The next morning I jumped out of bed with anticipation to check out my catch. To my dismay there were hundreds of little gar fish, and they were so tangled up in the net it was impossible to get them out of it without seriously damaging it. Once I got the fish out, I had an idea of what to do with them. I had a little garden spot that I had almost ready to plant. I took these fish and laid them end to end in a deep trench. I then covered them up and planted my garden over the fish. I thought this would be great fertilizer. It worked great until the garden was up about five inches and the fertilizer got to smelling so much that the coons found them. They dug up every plant in the garden.

We considered gar fish trash fish. So, we would try and eliminate them whenever we could. One night I had been fishing up the river and a very large gar took half of a nice fish I had caught. As the boat swung around, he came right up to me. I was very unhappy with him. I took my gig[1] and although he bent it, I managed to get him in the boat. The gig I used was home made. The tines were made out of very big fishhooks. I would straiten them and weld them to a base that could be replaced. The hooks went all the way through him. When I got back to the cabin, I left him in the boat. I wanted to show him off because of his size. He was a little under six feet.

During the night, a coon had found him and ate a fist size hunk right behind his head. After I finished showing him off it was about ten o'clock. He was gathering flies so I pushed him off into the river. He was floating and got caught up in an eddy current that caused him to circle around right behind the boat. I took the end of the boat paddle and was trying to push him away. Then I noticed his gills were moving, so I took the fishing pole and tried to pull him back. When I touched him he swam off into deep water like he was not hurt at all. That's why they have been around since the dinosaurs roamed the earth. He's probably still out there eating fish and telling how he got away.

---

[1] A spearlike device with a long, thick handle, used for spearing fish and frogs.
http://www.thefreedictionary.com/gig

COON CATCH

Little Hell Boat Landing on the Savannah River was the closest place for me to launch a boat. I had a boat that that I had built in my shop class at school. It was a racing design that I had found in a Popular Science magazine. I had a twelve HP Powermatic Wizard outboard motor that I had souped up and modified the prop. It was a lot faster than stock. My friend Ronald Barnett lived in Jackson, SC and they had a Yellow Jacket Boat with a big motor for skiing. The Savannah River Plant was between Barnwell and Jackson. The plant was closed to through traffic. This made the river the closest route. They had an event at the Jackson boat ramp that included boat racing, food, swimming and games. Me and a friend, Tommy Spencer, who also had a similar racing boat, decided to go up river to the event.

The boats were equipped with a dead man's throttle, which cut the motor back to idle when released. We were skipping along at a pretty good clip, when we saw a coon swimming the river. I cut the throttle back and approached the coon, picked him up by his tail and put him in a corn sack that I had in the boat. After I had tied the sack securely at the top, I placed it out of the way underneath the forward deck. We soon got back up to speed and went on down to the event. While racing in my class, I was running second and closing. There was a kid floating on a one-gallon oilcan. The wake of the previous boat filled the can and the boy couldn't swim. When I realized what was going on, I released the throttle and jumped in. I swam to the boy, got him and took him to shore. I think he might have drowned had I not rescued him. I lost the race, but we still had a great time.

We started back home that afternoon. About halfway home, I had forgotten all about the coon. He had chewed his way out of the sack. I was sitting holding the steering wheel and his head came out between my legs. I jumped up and the motor automatically cut back. The coon went to the back corner of the boat and was about to jump when I grabbed him by the tail again. This was not a very smart thing to do because the coon had a hold of the side of the boat. His head was about one inch from my stomach and he was trying to bite me. After three or four moments of this, my arms were getting very tired and he was as strong as I was. Finally, I let go and jumped back at the same time. Fortunately, he went for the corner of the boat to jump out instead of after me. He jumped back into the river and swam to shore with my blessings. That was an experience I'll never forget.

A PRESENT FOR BUCK

Roy Ratliff and I were driving home late one night from south Florida passing through a low swampy area not far from St. Augustine. There was no other traffic, but it was a little foggy so I was only driving about forty-five MPH. I saw the reflection of eyes in the ditch on my right. When I got closer, I saw that it was a large alligator and he jumped up and started running across the road in front of me. I went all the way over in the left lane to try and avoid him. In spite of my effort, I ran over his head.

When I managed to stop, I decided to back up and check him out. I put my headlights on him and walked in front of the car to get a closer look. Although he didn't have a mark on him he was graveyard dead. I decided to back the car up to him and take him home with me. He was about seven feet long and very heavy. It was all we could do to get his head in the trunk of the car. I took a rope and tied his tail to the bumper, then tied the trunk lid down so I wouldn't lose him on the way home. When I got home an hour or so later, I pulled into the driveway and took him out of the trunk. The St. Augustine grass on the front lawn was about four inches high. We drug him a few feet into the grass and left him there.

I took my overnight bag and went inside the house where I was greeted by the family and my brother Buck. After a few moments, I asked Buck if he had a flashlight that I could borrow. He got a flashlight and I told him that I had dropped my car keys in the grass and needed to find them. I took the flashlight and walked out in the grass. I got down on my hands and knees and started parting the grass looking for keys. He got down beside me and was helping me look. Little by little, I led him closer to the alligator. When I got him about two feet from the alligator's head, I shined the light on it. Buck screamed and gave me the front yard. Thus, I evened the score for some of the many things he had done to me in the past. We also skinned the alligator out and had some tasty alligator tail to eat for a while.

THIS LOOKS LIKE THE ONE

VACATION WITH ROLF ROWLS

My friend Rolf and I rode motorcycles to work. We had one week that we could take off work for a vacation once a year. This year we planned to tour the mountains. We left my house early in the morning. We each had sissy bars on the back of our motorcycles and we would tie our sleeping bags, bedrolls and other supplies to the sissy bars. This would also give us something to lean back on and make for a more comfortable ride.

Rolf had just bought a new larger and faster motorcycle than mine and was giving me a hard time about the fact. He was saying I wouldn't be able to keep up with him. I told him he could run off and leave me but if he did, he would be a scared SOB. He would blast by me and run up the road, I'd stay back because I didn't want to push him too hard. We still were making record time. We had left at 7 AM and were in Pikeville, Kentucky before dark, and this was before Interstate Highways went that way. We traveled Highway 23 through Georgia and when you cross the North Carolina - Tennessee line; it's on the top of the mountain. Just over the mountain, the road makes a sharp turn to the right. There's a little overlook there where you could spit a half mile if you were so inclined. Rolf didn't know the road, I had been over it before, and I remembered this.

Well sir he went tearing up the mountain wide open. I cautiously followed him expecting to see him free falling down the overlook. However, he and his motorcycle were laying on the side of the road about five feet from the drop off. He was white as a ghost and said, "Boy I almost didn't make that!"

I said, "I don't see how you did." After a few moments, he settled down and we started on our way, still at a rapid pace. Before dark, we checked into a motel in Pikeville. We had some friends there who came down to see us at the Motel. The first thing Rolf wanted to know was where the liquor store was. He was told that this was a dry county and the nearest one was in the last county he came through. They would still be open for a couple more hours. Our friend told him that he could borrow their car and go back there. So off he went.

The store was on the only flat place in the area. There was about a mile of straight flat road in front of it. When he went in the store, the owner was talking to another customer. He was telling him about some nuts that had come past the store on motorcycles earlier that day. He said, "I'll bet they were doing ninety miles per hour."

Rolf asked, "Was one of them red and the other one blue?"

He said, "How did you know?"

Rolf said, "That was me and my buddy, we left Jacksonville, Florida this morning at 7 AM and rode all day." Now if that was me, I don't think I would have told that! That was just the way Rolf was.

We spent a couple days in the area and started back in the direction of Atlanta. Rolf had a sister who lived there that he planned to see on the way back. We rode until we were tired then we would find a nice place to camp out. We would build a campfire, roll out the sleeping bags, fix some food and spend the night. We did this about three times and we were enjoying the trip but we were getting close to where we would get on the main road to Atlanta. It got very foggy and we were not able to go over twenty miles an hour. To make matters even worse, it got very cold in the mountains and we were about to freeze.

We decided to stop and build a fire and spend the night. We took the first cut off we came to which was a little two rut road that went to the left. By this time the fog was so bad we could only see right in front of us, maybe five feet. There was a pond that we almost ran into, but as soon as we stopped, there was an awful smell, somethings rotten! We started back out the road and there was another fork in the road so we took it. This seemed much better. We rode right up on a bunch of cardboard boxes and brush for firewood. Before long, we had a fire to warm by and cardboard to put our sleeping bags on. We settled in and went to sleep. The next morning when I woke up, I looked up at the smoke going up from the remains of our fire. It was one of those perfectly still mornings where the smoke went straight up for about a hundred feet then flattened out and went both directions. It just hung there. When I came to my senses I looked around and there was a line of traffic about thirty feet away from us bumper to bumper going into town. We were in the city dump.

The people were really checking us out. We had not shaved for a week and looked mighty grubby. When we got home, we told the guys at our office "We stayed in nice places most of the time but one night we stayed in a real dump." They didn't know how true that really was.

We planned to get to Rolf's sister's place that night. I didn't know the address, phone number, last name or anything. I was just following Rolf. It was after dark and raining when we got to the edge of Atlanta and my headlight on the motorcycle burned out. I had to keep him in sight and I couldn't see anything for the rain and backwash from the traffic. He said that he thought that I had turned my light off on purpose so I could sneak up on him. It's a miracle I wasn't killed! The good Lord was surely looking after me.

The next day I bought a new light and installed it. The rest of our trip was uneventful. I was very glad to be home safe and sound, but with lots of experiences that I wouldn't want to repeat.

UNCLE HORRIS

I had been playing with my band in and around Jacksonville, Florida for a few years. Everywhere we would play, they would want you to play something for everybody. Now this meant a little Rock, a little Folk and some Country. This usually resulted in the audience being lukewarm to your performance. I thought that it would be better to play one type of music. So when I got the opportunity to move to The State Line Lounge, near the Florida Georgia line I jumped at it. The owners were two brothers Troy and R. B. Lloyd. They had just bought the property in Nassau County, Florida and wanted the same thing. They wanted to pay a lot less than I wanted for my band. I made them a proposition, "If you let me play what I want to play for one month, I will work for what you want to pay. At the end of the month, if you're not satisfied, we will go our separate ways. But, if it's working you will pay me what I ask for." They agreed to this and we started playing Country Music. The first week, the people who came in were split. The Rock and Rollers, went away unhappy with what we were doing, as did the Folk fans. But the Country people, left very happy and told all their friends about us. The next week they brought their friends, so at the end of the third week the crowd was applauding every song. Standing ovations were common; they loved it!

It goes without saying that Troy and R B, came up with the funds and payed us what we wanted. The crowds continued to grow and they enlarged the building three times over the few years that we played. I have seen lines standing in the rain waiting to get in when we took our first break. One night I came in and they wanted to see me in their office. I thought one of the band members had done something wrong. When I got in their office, they gave me a bonus check and told me that they had paid off their mortgage the day before. They said it was largely because of my suggestion to play County Music. That sure made my day. I was glad to know I was appreciated.

Let me say here that the brothers loved to pull practical jokes. I made arrangements to have someone fill in for me to take a two week vacation. The last night I came to play before starting my vacation I got a speeding ticket. Nassau County was known for being a speed trap at the time anyway. This put me a little late getting to work at the club. When I came in Troy, said, "You're running a little late tonight aren't you?" I told him yes, I was, and I couldn't afford to come up there and play unless he would call off his dogs and stop them from giving me speeding tickets. He said, "Did you get a speeding ticket?" He said, "Let me see it." He said, "R.B., Uncle Horris gave him a speeding ticket. Who is the magistrate that you have to go before? Oh! That's our bookkeeper. Just give me the ticket and I'll take care of it." Well with that I forgot about it and went on my merry way and enjoyed my vacation.

When I returned to work, I was met at the door and he said, "Boy we're in trouble. Rather I mean you're in trouble." I asked why. He said Uncle Horris died and they transferred his cases to another Judge. I went and talked to him, but he was not at all understanding. He wants to see you as soon as you get back.

With this, I smell a practical joke coming on so I said, "Well I wished a lot of bad things on him, but I didn't think they would come true."

He said, "No I'm serious; he really did die." Well the next day I went to see the Judge. He was, as they said, not at all understanding. While I was sitting in his office he received several phone calls the last of which I heard him say, "Yes Sheriff Ellis I'll take care of it."

When we got back to our business I asked, "Was that Larrie Ellis?"

He said, "Yes, do you know Sheriff Ellis?"

I said, "I do, I used to go hunting with him. We have been friends for a long time."

With that, he seemed to mellow somewhat and finally said that I could pay court costs and he would dismiss it. And that is what I did.

THE ROAD TO NASHVILLE, GA

My wife's folks were all from Nashville, Georgia and they all still lived in that area. She had gone to spend Christmas week there and because of my work, I had to go up later. I drove my old 1965 Dodge pickup. A week or so before I made this trip, I had hauled some roofing shingles across town to a job I was doing on the side. They had loaded me up with a front-end loader. I could tell right away it was quite a load but I thought, I don't have far to go so I went with it.

The next time I drove the truck was the day after Christmas. I was on my way back home so I could go to work at midnight. About nine thirty that night, I was approaching Homerville, Georgia when I saw smoke coming from the back of my truck. There was a little store on the right that still had some lights on so I pulled off the road there. Before I rolled to a complete stop, the rear end locked up and I slid to a stop. I got out and with a flashlight and grease rag, and got under the truck to investigate the problem. The rear end was so hot you couldn't touch it. After it cooled some, I removed the filler plug and discovered there was not a drop of oil in it.

The little store didn't sell motor oil, rear end grease or anything like that. The only thing they had was Wesson cooking oil. I bought all three bottles that they had. When I started pouring it in, I could see a little hairline crack in the housing and the oil started slowly dripping out.

When I got all the oil in, I knew I would be losing oil on my trip and it would be a race to get home before it all ran out. I had to rock the truck backwards to get the rear end to break loose and roll forward. When I got back on the road, there was no traffic at all and I put it in the wind. A mile or so before I got home the smoke came back and when I rolled up in my yard, the rear end locked up and I again slid to a stop. I jumped on my motorcycle and made it to work on time. I sure was tired, but fortunately, the rest of the night was a lot slower.

On another occasion, I had gone to Nashville to visit again and someone told me about a guy that had a 426 Hemi engine in a barn that he wanted to sell. I thought this highly unlikely but it was worth investigating. I was into building racecars and this was the best and most sought after engine of all. One chance in a million but there it was covered with hay and other trash; man, what a find. I worked out a deal and bought it. The guy that had told me about it had an old two wheel trailer frame that he said I could borrow and return the next time I came up. We tied the engine to the frame and I started home.

On the way back, the right tire went flat. I didn't have a spare and I couldn't leave the engine on the side of the road, so I just continued to drive slowly. I kept the tire on the grass whenever I could. Some of the time, you just had to run on the pavement. Even doing this, the tire wore completely off the rim. I figured I would just buy the guy another rim from the salvage yard. I made it home OK and put my engine in the garage. After the holidays were over, I went to the salvage yard to get a rim. No one had a rim like that. It had metal spoke wheels They couldn't even identify what kind it was. After going to every salvage yard within a fifty-mile radius, still no luck. There was a body shop that had a few old junk vehicles out behind the business that I passed on the highway. I decided to stop and ask there. The owner didn't have any ideas either. There was an old man there that was also looking for parts he said, "I know what it is. It's off of a 1931 Studebaker Panel Truck. I have some of them at my place that I could sell you." Now what's the chance of that? I took my old tattered rim and followed him to his place and sure enough, he knew exactly what he was talking about. There they were and they even had the tires on the rims. He gave me a good price so I bought two of them. Now the trailer owner has a spare tire.

THIS IS WHAT I FOUND IN A BARN IN NASHVILLE, GA
COVERED WITH A TARP AND BURIED IN HAY

1931 studebaker panel truck

THE MIDDLEBURG RUN

One of our main things to do on weekends was to get in our cars and cruise down Main Street, and show them off. Now my car didn't have a radical cam that would make it lope, so I would pat the accelerator. This would flood the carburetor and make it sound as if it did have a radical cam. It would be washed and shined and looking great! On this particular night, Wayne Dunn and I had gone down to Middleburg from Jacksonville to pick up two girls we had recently met.

My car, a 1958 Plymouth 2 door hardtop with a big Chrysler motor, would always have way too much horse power for the three speed manual transmission to handle. Our destination was Ebb's Restaurant on North Main Street. We always measured our wealth in Ebb's steak sandwiches.

We would bet two steak sandwiches that this or that would happen. We had made our run to Ebb's and then across the street to Bailey's, where they had the girls roller skate to your car and serve you. There were Hickory nuts in the parking lot that caused trouble at times. All in all it was lots of fun.

We were still cruising Main Street when some guy got along side of us and kept trying to pick a race. After two or three red lights of this, I'd had enough so I floored the accelerator and you could hear all the teeth shearing off the gears and we just sat there. I looked at Dunn, and said, "Feller, I broke it!" He broke out in a big laugh. I still had second and high gear so we managed to take our dates home and get back home ourselves. This little episode destroyed the low and reverse sliding gear, the reverse idler gear and the cluster gear. The repairs took most of my pay for that week.

Wayne Dunn had a 57 Plymouth that he called Big Mama. I put a torque flight transmission in it for him. The way I did it was easy. I pulled the engine and put it together then put the whole thing back in. We took it out one night for a trial run. Wayne was up on 21st street and kicked it down just before a railroad crossing. When we hit the railroad crossing, we heard a big bang the headlights went out. He couldn't steer it and the brake pedal went to the floor when he tried to stop. Wayne was yelling, "What did you do to my car? I think the motor just fell out!" He was really upset with me! I didn't know what had happened but I was sure I had done it right.

After we pulled it home to my garage and we had time to investigate a little closer, what had really happened was a recapped tire that Wayne had on the right front had come loose and wrapped around the inside of the hub so he couldn't steer it. It had also broken the hydraulic brake line so it wouldn't stop. The recap had also hit the back of the headlight shorting the circuit and blowing the fuse to the lights. These true-life stories are sometimes stranger than fiction.

One of my sidelines was bodywork and painting cars. Back then, I would paint your car for one hundred dollars. This gave me a little extra spending money and I could buy the paint and supplies I needed for the job for about thirty dollars.

The girl that I had dated in Middleburg had bought a brand new Ford but she didn't like the color. She had wanted a fire engine red car but she had gotten such a deal on this car that she bought it anyway. She asked me if I would paint it fire engine red for her. I painted it red a perfectly beautiful job. I was so proud of it.

I notified her that I had it ready. She said she would meet me in a newly built shopping center that night. They had the first mercury vapor lights that I ever saw. They changed the color of everything they shined on and the car looked like canary crap. The girl was livid. She said that was not the color she had wanted. I tried to explain that it was not really the color it was, but she went on and on. Needless to say I didn't get payed that night. However, the following day she called me and was sorry she hadn't paid me and she did. Everything turned out OK after all.

STRICKLAND'S LANDING

From Jacksonville, if you travel right on through Middleburg you will come to Kingsley Lake.

There were two main access points for the public to get to the lake to enjoy it. Both had rides, slides and dance halls with bands playing music. I had played music at both. I was now playing at Strickland's Landing and my friend Wayne Dunn usually went with me. Voluptuous girls in bikini bathing suits danced all day and into the night to our music.

Wayne liked to sing a few songs with the band. He was particularly fond of Jimmy Reed, a black singer, so he would sing one of his songs. This night it was almost closing time and one bikini-clad girl was dancing all alone. She was at the other end of the dance floor when Wayne started his rendition of Jimmy Reed. Her eyes were focused on him as she danced closer and closer.

The closer she got the more nervous Wayne got. She danced right up on the stage. Wayne couldn't stand any more so he abandoned the microphone. Poor Wayne, what a way to be run off stage.

One time I was driving to my job at Strickland's Landing; it was raining and had been for some time. The road was flooded and I was running a little late so I was pushing the speed limit to the

leading edge. I was driving my 1964 356 Porsche SC when I hit a flooded place in the road and spun around going off the road to the right. I managed to regain some control and get it headed in the right direction. Then I realized if I stopped, I would be stuck so I gave it the gas with the tires spinning slinging mud everywhere I made it back to the highway and continued on my way. When I got to work, I discovered I was missing a hubcap. It was dark when I got off work so I didn't try to find it that night. The next morning I went to the place I had lost it. To my surprise, there was a large ditch about fifteen feet wide and six feet deep that I had crossed over and back. I could see the car tracks and my hubcap was on the far side of the ditch. The bottom of my car had planed on the water due to my speed and kept me from sinking. The good Lord was surely looking out for me!

WE'VE BEEN INVADED

I was working out of the Jax Radio Office. One Friday night I had been playing music late and had just gotten home. It was about 2AM and my phone was ringing when I walked in the door. It was Pearly Felts, one of my coworkers. He said ,"Meet me at Jax Radio ASAP." I jumped back in my car and took off for the station. When I got there, he was sitting in an L truck with the motor running. I had thought that we must have Radio trouble, but L Trucks were used for L Coax underground cable issues.

He said, "We've got a total L 3 failure up north. That's over one hundred thousand circuits. The trouble has been isolated to a section of the Atlanta cable route." We were on route to the problem area and turned off the main road onto a two-rut road going towards the cable right of way. It had been raining for a couple of weeks and the road was under water. We only managed to go a short distance before the truck got stuck. We took a few things we needed in hand and waded back to the right of way.

When we got to the right of way, we started north toward the section that the office gurus had said the trouble was located. The land there was slightly above the water but when we got there, the evidence was obvious. There was a large pine tree that had been struck by lightning. It looked as if a huge hog had rooted from the tree to the cable and stopped. Pearly, said, "This is where we dig." The dirt here was such that you could take a shovel full of dirt and the sand would fill the hole back up like beach sand. So, we got some lumber from the L truck to shore up the sides as we dug. We also went and got a mud pump so we could pump out water and mud as we dug as well. After a couple hours of this, we had exposed the cable enough for us to work on it.

The cable is about three inches in diameter and contains coax tubes and paper pairs. Each had to be spliced individually. Where the lightning had hit the cable, it looked like someone had placed it on a railroad track and flattened it out with a sledgehammer. We cut the section out and spliced it. The ends of the splice had to be sealed by pouring melted lead into a fiber form that we made. The cable itself was armored metal with a plastic sheath over that. With that repair done, we still had a problem.

The lighting had run down the cable for about twenty feet and where it left the cable, it was flattened in the same way. We therefore, had to repeat the process once again. The office had called in a contractor and other office personal to help us by the time we made the second splice. We had

41

been on the job for more than twenty-four hours and surely needed some relief. We got some food and some much-needed rest. Our operations manager even gave us a pocketknife for our extra effort.

A few months after this job, Pearly and I were working on a cable modification south of Jacksonville. We would go in to work at midnight in order to have the least possible interruption of service. We gained access through manholes, which were one mile apart. We would each get into one and talk to the other on a telephone wire connecting the two of us. We would then patch service to the spare tube and modify it, then patch another one off and repeat the process. Pearly was not familiar with the fact that the cable right of way was on an old military base. To get to it, we had to unlock the gate and then we were on the base.

About daybreak, the fog was beginning to lift a little and Pearly stuck his head out to see the world. He was greeted by army tanks crashing all around him and military troops running around jabbering in a foreign language. He yelled to me on the line, "Man, we're being invaded!" The U. S. Army was in the process of training Vietnamese Army Troops. Pearly was in panic mode for a while until he learned the rest of the story.

SAFETY MEETING

Every month or so we would be called in for a safety meeting; although other things deemed important were also discussed. The meeting was slated to start at 9:30 AM. I arrived at 8 AM so I could talk to some of the guys that I only saw at these meetings. There was a guy named Steve that was doing bench work, repairing units. It was a job that I had for a year or so, maybe two years earlier. I went over to his workbench and was talking to him. He was working on a 400 CPS power supply for aircraft use. I asked Steve if he had it under control. He said he did and had parts on order to repair it. I had seen this same trouble many times and I said, "Steve, that's not going to be your trouble." About that time, my boss, James walked up and Steve told him that I didn't think that would fix the trouble. James assured me that it would. I said, "I don't think so."

James said, "I'll bet you a steak dinner at one of the local restaurants." I agreed to the bet and forgot all about it. A couple of months later when I returned for the next meeting, the entire office was aware of the bet. They had held the part so we could all witness the instillation. After the meeting, they were going to show me the repair.

The Lake City, Florida office was about twenty miles away, and I had a friend Jessie Lamb that was coming to the meeting also. I asked him if he had a matched pair of PNPN gated diodes. He said he did and I asked him to bring them to me. He gave me the diodes when he got to the office and I put them in my pocket. After the meeting everyone came over and watched Steve replace the parts he and James had ordered. The same trouble was there as before. I gave Steve the gated diodes from my pocket and pointed out the ones to replace. He did and when they turned it on, it worked perfectly. James shook his head said, "You just can't beat Tripp's intuition." I really enjoyed my steak dinner!

The cost of fuel was creeping up more and more, so the head honchoes up the road made a decision to restrict our driving. It was mandated that we go to only one station per day. The first day of this new mandate, I had a tower lighting alarm in one of my stations. I went to that tower and discovered a bad Crouse Hines rocker switch. I called in to the office and was told that the tower at Archer, Florida had a switch that was no longer required and I could get that one the next day. The tower I was in had just had all the routine tests done three days earlier so there was not much I could do.

The next day I removed the switch from Archer tower and did what other tests I could. The third day when I got back to the original trouble, the switch was different and wouldn't work. Here I was now four days behind in my work with no improvements in sight. There were three of us covering all the radio towers in North Florida. How could you get more efficient than that? The extra station visits were from passing by on the way to another station. When time permitted, I would run and make a quick inspection. This way I could catch a weak transmitter before it went into alarm. In the end, I think it would have been more efficient to just let us do our jobs.

BEACON 16

Let me first say that each morning or sometime during the day, I ask my lord and savior Jesus Christ for guidance to meet the challenges of the day. This period would prove to be a very challenging time in my life. Jacksonville Beach was like a carnival at the time. At the south end of the beach was a place called Beacon 16. There was a wide concrete boardwalk where you could look up the beach and see that it curved to the right. It was totally lined with businesses, roller coasters, three Ferris wheels, dodge um cars; you name it, it was there.

For a few months, I had been playing my guitar and singing in Beacon 16. People could walk in off the boardwalk, enjoy the music and spend their money on the game machines, souvenirs or snacks. With the large military presence there, it was the perfect place for the sailors to unwind after a long cruse. One ship from Mayport Carrier Base could put thousands of customers on the beach.

It was common practice for my band to leave all their instruments and amplifiers in the club, because we played there every night. On the weekends, we played all day. The others would laugh at me because I would load up my guitar, amplifier and microphone every time I left the club. I always took them with me. I realized it was a lot of trouble but it made me feel better.

I was working for AT&T, so when hurricane Dora came up the coast, I knew I would be busy for a while. Hurricane Dora not only came up the coast, it came in at Jacksonville Beach. When it made landfall it stopped and made no movement for over 48 hours. This meant that high tide came in several times in 120 MPH winds.

After it moved on, I was sent to the beach to try and restore phone service. When I arrived, the surf was breaking on 5th Ave. I could see a couple of houses floating out in the ocean. There was not one thing left standing on the first three blocks from the ocean. The water was still so high I could do little to restore service. A ship had broken loose from its mooring in Jacksonville and it had drug its anchor, hooking our L cable lying on the bottom of the river. I was sent to assist in laying a new cable across the river. It had to be spliced at both ends and plowed under the bottom of the river. This we accomplished in about a week, record time for such a job. Eventually things got back to normal. A crew was sent down from Atlanta and Bell Labs to show us how to modify one of our L cables that ran along the river south of Jacksonville.

These guys had all the answers. They had some new improvements for the cable route and were anxious to share their brilliance with us. They were unhappy with us taking so much time to work on that cable. The manhole covers were about ten inches above the ground level. These manholes were four feet wide and eight feet long. When you got inside, you had enough room to remove the pressurized covers from the equipment and do your job. These guys got to work in earnest about ten in the morning, although they were in the planning stage earlier. With the manhole open, they took a lunch break and left at about twelve o'clock. Unfortunately, they didn't realize they were in the tidal basin. When they returned, the tide had come in and the entire thing was under water. The reason for us taking more time was in fact because we could only work on those manholes at low tide. Total recovery from the storm damage as far as communications would take a major redesign.

The radio tower and building at Jacksonville Beach was flooded beyond repair. A new building and tower would be built a couple miles north of the old site on higher ground. I didn't get involved in this until after it was built. I was working radio at the Jacksonville number 2 office. The four-story building took up a quarter of the block. I have been accused of being facetious at times and not without cause. My repair room had a microwave dummy load antenna, which consisted of a wave guide that went up the wall then weaved back and forth across the ceiling long enough for it to develop its characteristic impedance.[2] This was about sixty feet. At the base of the antenna, I had hung a roll of solder, so I could just pull off a little when I was making repairs and needed it. My boss came in one day and said it didn't look very good and asked if I could do something about it. I found a metal box about five by five by four inches that had two push button switches on the front of it. After cutting out the top and mounting it so it would fit over my roll of solder, I removed the bottom switch' installed a rubber grommet and fed the end of my solder through the hole. This was ascetically pleasing to my boss. I could now just reach up and pull out a little solder whenever I needed it.

A few weeks after this, I was working on a transmitter using the dummy load antenna for alignment when someone came by conducting a guided tour of the radio room. The guide got distracted for a moment and the greenhorns were asking me questions about my operation. I tried as best I could to explain what I was doing. When they asked about my solder box, I told them it was a solder dispenser. To demonstrate how it worked I reached up and pushed the button and pulled out on the solder. Then I said, "If I get a little too much, I just push the button again and I pushed the solder back in." They thought it was motorized. I had a speaker on an order wire (a speaker that everyone could hear) so I could talk to other locations in the building. You couldn't see the speaker

---

[2] The effective resistance of an electric circuit or component to alternating current, arising from the combined effects of ohmic resistance and reactance. Google

but you could hear impulse noise from crosstalk of the telegraph lines. This is where the real dig comes. They looked up at that antenna weaving back and forth across the ceiling, and asked what it was and why it was making that noise. I told them that the solder had to be specially treated for microwave applications and we were treating a ten-year supply of solder that was contained in the waveguide. After they left, the word came back to me how amazed they were in the radio room, especially how we had to treat the solder for microwave applications.

As I mentioned previously, because of that same hurricane, a new microwave station and tower was built on the beach farther north on a little higher ground. However when it came time to turn up service on it, it did not meet specifications. While trying to solve the problem I discovered two major issues. One was that the dehydrators feeding dry air to the antennas on our building were insufficient. When we got a rain shower during the hot summer, it would cool the antennas so fast that I had seen the pressure gage show a negative reading. Being the facetious person that I was, I found a plastic chrome looking water facet and glued it to the bottom of the waveguide where it came out of the dehydrator. Of course, any penetration of the waveguide would really mess it up. When the gurus came to assess the problem, I thought they were going to have a heart attack. I told them I had installed it to drain the water out of the system. Of course, it was a joke that they found little humor in.

The other problem I discovered when I had gone to the top of the building and with a good telescope I could see the tower at the beach. I could see that it barely missed the Embers Steakhouse on the top floor of one of the nearby buildings. I could also see that it was shooting through the bridge at Commodore's Point. I reported my findings and they asked how I had determined this. I said, "The Steakhouse patrons were complaining about their steaks being too done and the signal was worse during bridge high traffic hours."

It turned out that I was right on both counts. The engineers wanted to raise the tower high enough to shoot over the bridge, but they were told the building wouldn't support the additional weight. At the time, the building was four stories high and took up a quarter of the block. The remedy turned out to be to build the building eight stories high and take the whole block. Then put a tall tower on the new part. This worked fine but was unfortunately very expensive.

FLORIDA HIGHWAY PATROL CONTRACT

I always enjoyed building racing engines. I also would take my car to the drag strips in our area and run it once in a while. I was working at the AT&T Office at 415 Clay Street and had to pay to park in a parking lot about three blocks north of the office. I had a three-block walk any way and in the afternoon in the summer, it was usually raining. That's a whole story all its own. I had bought a new 1969 Plymouth 440 GTX from a dealer about three blocks from where I worked. There were quite a few problems with the car that were going to be fixed by the dealer. I was told to bring the car in and leave it with them in the morning and they would fix it during the day. Each afternoon when I got off work, I would return to pick up my car. And each day, they would profusely apologize for not getting it done. However, they would be glad to try again tomorrow. This went on for five weeks.

I'm sure they thought I'd just give up after a while and fix it myself since the guys in the shop knew that I did mechanic work on the side. Then one afternoon I told them not to worry about that because it kept me from paying parking and I had to walk about the same distance to work anyway. The very next afternoon everything was fixed perfectly. A few weeks later, I had driven up to North Carolina to visit my dad. On the way back, the engine developed a skip. I checked it out when I got home and found that a head gasket had blown between cylinders number five and seven.

I was taking a few vacation days off work but this car was still under warranty; so I took it to another one of their branches, Massey Mixon on Phillips Highway in South Side. They had about thirty-five mechanics working in the garage but there was only one building engines. While I was standing around trying to get a schedule worked out, one of the mechanics recognized me from a racetrack encounter. He said, "There's you a mechanic, hire him."

The service manager asked if I was a mechanic. I told that I did a little mechanical work now and then. He said, "I'll hire you and you can fix your own car." That sounded like a deal I couldn't refuse. I explained that I had a job but I'd help him out for a little while. I was offered a salary or commission of forty percent of the labor. I took the commission because I didn't know how well I could perform on a per hour basis. As it turned out, I was the second highest paid mechanic at the dealership. The number one guy did transmission repair and he was the best I've ever seen at that job. He had a jig he had made with pressure regulators that would allow him to adjust a servo[3] to close at just the right pressure; no test drive necessary, it would work perfectly.

This dealership had the maintenance contract for the Florida State Highway Patrol vehicles. The cars were four-door with a special 440 cubic inch TNT interceptor engine and 292 ratio sure grip rear end. They would run what was on the speedometer — 160 MPH. Sometimes they would need that and more in pursuit on interstate 95. The Captain of the highway patrol was in there complaining that he had the slowest car on the force. He had been complaining for some time to the manager. The manager asked me if I could do something to make his car faster. I told him I could if I could order some parts that we didn't stock. He said, "Order whatever you need."

I ordered a special cam, valves lifters and springs. After installing all the new goodies and pulling a few special tricks, I had it running real good. I took it out on the interstate for a trial run. When you're driving a Highway Patrol car, you don't worry about the speed limit. I ran it up until it was completely out of numbers and it was still pulling strong. I backed it off and returned to the shop. I was sure he would be able to tell the difference.

He picked up his car and I didn't hear anything for a couple of weeks. Then I heard that there had been an accident on the interstate and he was in the hospital. Another trooper told us that he was in pursuit of a Boss Mustang and the car had passed the Captain siting in his car beside the road. He had joined the pursuit and had caught up with the Mustang. He was bumping the rear bumper of the Mustang and they both spun out and crashed their cars. They said the first thing he said when they went to see him in the hospital was, "Don't you let anybody take the engine out of my car. When I get another one, I want that engine put in it." Luckily, no one was seriously injured.

---

[3] A Servo is a small device that incorporates a two wire DC motor, a gear train, a potentiometer, an integrated circuit, and an output shaft. Of the three wires that stick out from the motor casing, one is for power, one is for ground, and one is a control input line. Google

ELLISVILLE

I was working microwave radio out of Ellisville, Florida. Ellisville was where my boss was located. I had a company van, and Chiefland, Florida was where my office was located. My job involved taking care of microwave stations from the Georgia state line south to Polk City, Florida. Chiefland was a large office that was a hardened site and had a 225 KW V-twelve diesel. It was also fenced in with a chain link fence. I usually took the van home with me because I was on call twenty-four hours a day. I took a week's vacation and my boss wanted me to leave the van at Chiefland just in case someone needed to use it. On Monday morning after my vacation, I arrived at work and the gates were lying flat on the ground. They were still held together by a heavy chain and pad lock.

They were torn off the hinges and my van was gone. I called the police and my boss and reported my problem. The first thing my boss wanted to know was where the key to the van was. I told him and showed him it was in my pocket. It wasn't long until a couple of detectives arrived to investigate. They found where two people had climbed the fence and some glass where the window of the van was broken out. Then I overheard them saying, "Yes that's their mode of operations." It seems that two prisoners had broken out of prison a couple of miles away and made off with van.

We were very concerned about the test equipment in the van. It cost three times as much as the van itself. They found the van abandoned near Orlando the next day. They had broken out the window and hot-wired the ignition, but all the equipment was there plus a wristwatch with a broken band. The damage to the van was minimal, a broken light and a few dents in the front. We had a big meeting back in Ellisville to determine what I could have done to prevent this kind of thing from happening. I told them they could buy a big log chain and padlock and I could run it over the axle then lock it to the microwave tower.

Things always seemed to go wrong when I took a little vacation time. I returned from vacation and was called by my boss and told that I was needed in Chiefland ASAP. When I arrived, they had a portable generator pulled up close to the office and cables had been run inside to charge the batteries. They could not get the big generator to start. The power had failed and all the microwave channels were in low mo, or low microwave output. The portable generator wasn't enough to keep the building running and the power was slowly failing.

The power had failed on Friday and the generator had failed to start. All the bosses and all the technicians they could round up were there helping. They had been working on it all weekend and I had no idea what all they had done. As soon as I came in, I was handed a schematic and told to check out one of the circuits. I checked out the circuit that I was given and found nothing wrong with it. I was immediately given another and another right up until lunchtime. I always brought my lunch with me, so everyone left me alone. My boss James said, "Tripp, you ought to know how to fix this trouble; after all it's your office." So I continued to work on the problem until I discovered something had tripped the sensors. The building had flash, vibration, and radiation sensors. This was to seal up the building in case of a nuclear attack and would prevent contamination from being pulled into the building. Sometimes a lightning flash or a sonic boom would trigger this. It would have to be reset manually. I reset it and the big diesel started perfectly. When they returned from lunch, I had everything back to normal. James asked what I had done. I said I fixed it! He asked me what was wrong with it. I said, "Nothing it worked just like it is supposed to."

FLORIDA AIR NATIONAL GUARD

When I turned twenty-one, mandatory draft was in effect and all males were required to serve in the military. I signed up and was soon on my way to San Antonio, Texas for basic training.

The one and only time I flew during my six years of service was on a commercial airplane from Jacksonville to Tampa to Dallas. Then we were put on a military DC 3 the remainder of the way.

The DC 3 flew very low to the ground. There were six new inductees on the flight and we sat on the floor with the side cargo door open. When we arrived, we were immediately put in formation and assigned to a cursing, hell-raising, fire-breathing drill instructor. He called us rainbows because our cloths were all colors. He also let us know that he had a dislike for all rainbows and we were lower than whale shit! Later that day we stood in a line in our shorts getting vaccinations in both arms.

Then, we got a one-month in advance paycheck. They cashed it and as we progressed down the line, they said you need this, and this, and this. At the end of the line, you had uniforms, two pair of boots, towels, toothbrush, three-piece razor, some dial soap and they had all of your money. Then you were marched off to the barracks and the training squadron you were assigned to. For the next sixteen weeks, you never got more than two hours of uninterrupted sleep. The nights were filled with fire drills, forced nighttime marches, and anything they could come up with to interrupt your sleep.

One night a drill instructor from the squadron next door came to our door and demanded the guard on duty let him in. The airman on guard duty would not open the door. The drill instructor screamed, "You dip shit, open this G D door or I'm gonna kick your ass." This created such a commotion that the entire barracks was awake. Finally, under pressure, the guard let him in. Then he started jumping up and down screaming our drill sergeant's name saying that "this dumb son of a bitch" let me in your barracks.

Our Sargent came running in yelling, "Throw that asshole out of my barracks."

The guard started toward the invader when he pulled out a pocketknife and said, "I'll cut you, you M F." Our Sargent was still yelling, "Throw him out!" The biggest and strongest man in our squadron came and grabbed him by the back of the neck and seat of his pants, and threw him out the front door. This kept us all awake for a few hours. From then on, when we would march past our neighboring squadron, this same guy, Charles Gold, would be first in line. The Sargent would cower down and say, "Keep that man away from me!"

Charles Gold and I became good friends, partly because he and I were in the best physical shape. Charles had been in a gymnastics team and could walk on his hands, do flips, tumble, and do all the things that go along with that. When we would run laps, he would be first, I would be a close second, while the rest of the field would be a long way back. When we ran four laps, they would be three quarters of a lap behind. I could walk on my hands, but he could run on his and do pushups while standing on his. I never did master that.

One day a drill Sargent passed me. I was preoccupied and failed to salute him. Our names were on our uniforms and he yelled, "Tripp! Give me twenty pushups."

I snapped to attention and said, "Sir! Would you like that ten with one arm and ten with the other or twenty with both arms?"

He broke out laughing. "You can't do a one armed pushup!" I jumped to the ground and did ten with one arm then ten with the other. I jumped back up, snapped to attention and saluted him. He just stood there with his mouth agape.

One night we had been out all night training and we were sitting on a ridge overlooking a valley about a quarter of a mile wide. No air was stirring and the valley was filled with fog. We were told to advance to the other side of the valley. When we reached the fog, we found it was actually tear gas. We had had tear gas training but we had no gas masks. We ran into trees and stumbled through the gas, but somehow made it out.

When I finally got out of basic training, they put us on a train to Lowery Air Force Base near Denver, Colorado. Our train went to Dallas where we sat for a day, until a different engine hooked up to our cars and we started up the Texas Pan Handle. It was in September and still hot in San Antonio. We all had short-sleeved 505 tan uniforms. We were in route for three days, but we finally left Texas, went through Oklahoma and into Colorado. When we got in Colorado, we began to see snow on the ground.

When we arrived in Colorado Springs, we were met by a chartered Greyhound Bus, which would take us to the base. The bus driver got us to the base and a guide got on the bus to direct him to the right barracks.

It was late at night and we were all tired and sleepy. After making several turns and driving a ways, the guide said, "Turn left just past that white elephant."

The bus driver stopped in the middle of the road, wiped both eyes, stared, and then said, "I don't see no white elephant!" We all learned then that the military referred to dumpsters as white elephants.

We were given a couple of blankets and assigned to a barracks. The barracks were heated by a coal-fired furnace. We learned later that one of our regular duties was fire duty, or firing the furnaces for the entire squadron. There were five barracks, so you would shovel coal into the firebox in the basement of each building. By the time you did this to all five barracks, it was time to start over.

Our barracks backed up to an airstrip and we were assigned to eat at a chow hall on the other side of it half a mile away. The temperature was twenty degrees and the wind was always blowing. We made this trip three times a day for the next three days in our short sleeve uniforms before we finally got our winter uniforms. I was supposed to go to Electronics School, so I had to wait until the next one started. While I was waiting, I was assigned to what they called a PATS Squadron, or Personnel Awaiting Training. This meant all kind of work duties. I had gotten a few letters from my friend Wayne Dunn, back in Jacksonville. He usually told me about dating my old girl friends and rubbing it in. He had the second highest score on the test we had taken and was slated for the next school opening. I had KP Duty and here he came, side stepping through the chow line. Very nervous, afraid to even look up, he held a tin tray and would stick it out when he came to something he wanted. Well he stuck it out when he came to me. I got the biggest gob of mashed potatoes that I could get in my serving spoon and hit his tray with it. He looked up, I was looking him in the eyes and said without moving my mouth, "You son of a bitch!" He just broke into a wide grin, glad to know he was with an old friend.

We soon started Basic Electronics School with about six hundred more students. The school was divided into blocks that covered one subject, usually lasted about two weeks long. Tests were given at the end of the block and if you failed the test, you started it over. If you failed it again, you were eliminated from the course. If you passed the second time, you went to the next block. If you failed three blocks like this, you were eliminated. After eleven and a half months of this, I was one of the few that had not been setback and graduated with thirty-six other students. We then were divided up and sent to different set schools. Some went to Vulcan Gun School, some went to Avionics School. I went to Missile Guidance Systems School.

After eleven and a half months of this, my class that started out with thirty-six soldiers had been cut to six. One of the missiles that I studied had a nuclear warhead so then I was sent to Nuclear Weapons School. You guessed it - for another eleven and half months.

Of course, when all this was going on, we had a lot of other things happening. We had a joker in our barracks that was continually pulling jokes on us. For instance, he would short sheet your bed. This is where your two sheets were taken off and folded in half and put back on your bed so when you went to get in bed at night your feet hit bottom about half way down and you couldn't get in. So we started to fight back. I remember we came in from town one night and he was already asleep. We started yelling, All right, get up; it's time to fall out!" He got out of bed half asleep went and shaved, got fully dressed before he realized it wasn't morning.

But! The very best thing we pulled on him was something better. We had this running battle with the barracks next door. We were all in bed asleep and I got up and went outside and got a trashcan filled with fresh snow, which was about twenty inches deep outside. I came back and one of the other guys pulled his sheet back and I dumped the snow in the bed with him. We both ran out the front door and around the building and came back in and went to bed. Meanwhile he had run out in his shorts thinking the guys next door were the culprits. He ran right into the CQ making his rounds and was hauled off to the orderly room where he sat like that for the rest of the night. It took him quite a while to explain what he was doing running around in the snow in his shorts at night.

We were off duty for a week or so around Thanksgiving, but we had no place to go. So we decided to have our own party. Beyond the last barracks, there had been a language school that had recently moved out. Five or six empty barracks seemed like a good place to party. Some of the guys went off base and slipped in a few cases of beer. It was below zero outside so we had to bring the beer inside to keep it from freezing. We threw the mattresses on the floor and we were lying around telling jokes and drinking beer. It occurred to somebody that it was about time for the CQ to make his rounds. However, no one thought he would make it down to these empty barracks.

Anyway, we were upstairs and we could hear if someone came in downstairs. We would just run out the back door fire escape. No sooner than that was said, we heard the door downstairs open and we sounded like a herd of cattle running for the back door. The back door was locked and we had no place to hide. We all got caught and were marched down to the orderly room. The Commanding Officer said we all should lose a stripe. Since it was a holiday, he decided to give us a break and we just received a little extra duty.

On Thanksgiving Day, some of us were invited to eat dinner by some nice people in the area. Ben Anders one of the best fiddle players I ever met, Wayne Dunn, Jack Even, Chester Wheeler and myself went to a nice home on the side of the mountains overlooking Denver. I took a guitar and Ben took his fiddle. We entertained everyone and had a wonderful meal.

A few weeks later Ben and I were on a Denver city bus going to a VFW to play. There was standing room only on the bus and we were standing right behind the bus driver. He asked us to play him a tune. We started playing a hoe down and everybody on the bus started clapping. The whole bus was rocking. When we got to the VFW, we were supposed to meet a couple more guys we had met before and had started playing with them. One of the guys had been Carl Perkins' bass player, and the other one had played drums for Jerry Lee Lewis. These were very good musicians and could play several instruments.

One night a patron asked for one of Carl Perkins' song. I said I knew it and I sang it. When I finished, the bass player said, "Dam Saunch, you sound more like Carl on that than he does."

One time we were off and decided to go ice-skating. Up in the area of Red Rocks west of Denver was a place called Evergreen on the Ice. This was an old volcanic lake that was frozen over. None of us had ever had ice skates on, though most of us could roller skate. How different could it be? More than we ever thought. We rented skates, got them on and found out our ankles wanted to flop in or out, but after a while, we learned to stand and skate slowly around the rink. We were just enjoying ourselves and noticed that everybody was leaving. They were running and leaving as fast as they could. We ask someone what was going on.  They said, "You'd better get out of here or you'll get snowed in." We took their advice and made hast to get our skates off. We were still the last ones to leave.

We started around the mountain road back and the snow was higher than my front bumper. We came to a place where the road was downhill for about one hundred yards then went up hill.

When we reached the uphill part, we started spinning our tires but not going anywhere. I would back up as far as I could then try to go forward. After doing this about five times, I finally got over the hill. It was very treacherous driving, but we made it back.

Another time the snow was too deep and was forecast to be a lot more, so they wouldn't let us take our cars off base. I had a date to go to a movie with a girl I had met. I took a bus to town and went to the movie with my girlfriend. When we got out of the movie, the snow was knee deep. She lived only a block or so from the movie theater so we walked to her house. After visiting a little while, I left, walking down town to find a bus or a taxi, only to find they had all stopped running. I had duty the next morning so I started walking the ten miles to base.

There was a big clock tower at the base of Colfax Street. It had a clock on all four sides, and it flashed time and temperature. You could see and read it for three or four blocks. I had to walk three blocks to it then turn left towards the base. It showed seventeen degrees when I started walking towards it. By the time I had made the turn and was looking back at it, the temperature had dropped to minus thirty degrees. I had on an overcoat and overshoes. I walked almost all the way to the base. I was about a mile away when a carload of airmen came by and yelled there was room for one more. I jumped in and we would continue until we lost traction. Then we would jump out, push and pile back in when we got traction again. I made it in on time. I found out next morning the temperature had dropped to minus forty degrees that night.

Next day I was walking to the post office. The sun was bright and there was a very clear blue sky. Your breath would fog and then turn to ice crystals and fall sparkling to the ground. I said to one of my friends, "Good morning," then reached out my gloved hands and caught the crystals. I held them out to show him and said, "Did you ever see what one of those looked like?"

MULTIPLEX SCHOOL

I got called into Ellisville to teach a multiplex routing and patching school. The school lasted three weeks and involved a lot of patching of hot service for routine maintenance. The smallest thing you could patch at this level was six hundred circuits, or a super group. The school went off without any interruptions of service and was over. One of my students asked one last question about patching and I very quickly put up a patch and explained it. The patch involved a bridging point, which caused the signal level going out to drop by three DB. The channel that I patched was going south to the Polk City alarm center. I heard him say on the order wire, "I just got a hit from Tampa."

I was laughing when James walked up and asked what I was laughing at. I said, "Polk City don't even know what system just took a hit." He got on the order wire and asked the tech at Polk City if he was sure it wasn't from Ellisville instead of Tampa.

He said, "Well yes, it was from Ellisville." James told him we just had a manmade error here. Now a manmade error involves a ton of paper work on each end of the section involved. It also instigates follow up meetings where the one that made the error must explain the reason for such a dastardly deed. I was hung out to dry by my boss and I explained it was kind'a like driving a keg of nails and being told not to hit your thumb. There's a good possibility that you might hit your thumb.

About a week after that meeting James was in the same area attempting to patch off a master group; 1800 circuits, except he put his patch in a jack that opened service. Alarm bells went off everywhere.

I said, "James, you can't patch that there!" He took the patch down and the alarms cleared. He thought about it then decided he was right and put it up again. All the alarms went off again. By this time, half of south Florida was on the order wire reporting that they had lost service. James told them we were experiencing incoming problems. He was still determined to prove he was right, and asked me "Where dose this cable go from here?" I told him and he said, "No it don't," and climbed up in the cable racks following the cable. He wanted me to follow him to prove his point. I went around to where I knew the cable went and waited. When he got above me, he started jerking on the cable and asked me, "Where is this cable going?"

I grabbed it, pulled back and asked, "Is this it?"

He said, "Yes, where is it going?"

I said, "Right here where I told you it went." He never admitted any fault in this service interruption even though he was totally responsible for it.

Soon after all of this, the powers that be in Atlanta and Bell Labs made a high level decision to further reduce our driving. We had a helicopter that flew the right of ways that our routes took, just in case they saw any heavy equipment work starting. They would land and inform them of our cable location. The new plan was for us to take our toolbox and the helicopter could drop us off at the tower we needed to work on at that day then pick us up on the way back and return us to the office. I knew my toolbox wouldn't have the part I needed for a repair so I thought this would be a good time for me to make a change. I put in for a transfer to North Carolina because I had a hundred acres of land that joined my sister's land there. James said he could get me a transfer to Southern Bell in Wilmington, NC if I would go to a Number One ESS School and then install one in Wilmington. Then I could always transfer back to AT&T later. AT&T still owned Southern Bell at this time so I saw no problem with this. He said after the switch is up and running you can transfer closer to home. This particular installation was a toll switcher needed for a new area code. It would be the first of its kind in North Carolina. The school however would be in Greensboro, NC, and it was about a year long. My land was near Sanford, NC, and Greensboro was a little closer than Wilmington, so that would work out fine. I moved my family up to my land in a travel trailer. I planned to live in it until I could build my house.

Sanford was a very small place at that time. There was nothing open after dark and the few places that opened on weekends closed at noon. Thus, I had a real problem trying to get building supplies or anything else I needed. I started cutting logs from some of the places I needed to clear. I would pull them out to a high dirt bank and park my flatbed trailer at the bottom. Then I would roll the logs off onto the trailer and take them to Doc Beal's sawmill. He would saw lumber for me and I would pick it up the next week and take him another load of logs. This kept me with enough lumber to work on the house when I was home for the weekend.

CAR RESCUES

Being the kind of guy who has an affinity for sturdy vehicles, I always have something that can retrieve a car from a bog or wherever it may stuck. From time to time, I have had the opportunity to rescue some travelers in distress. I left the cabin one morning going to Branford. As I crossed the river, I saw a car with a man hanging on to the rear bumper. There was a boat ramp along the side of the bridge where people would launch their boats. This guy had let his car get away from him and it had rolled into the water up to the windshield. The water was swift and the car was rocking. Any time it could go down river and be lost. I was driving an old Dodge Power Wagon four-wheel drive with a PTO wench on the front. I immediately pulled behind him and connected the cable from the wench. I put the truck in reverse and pulled him out.

This brings to mind another car rescue. For this story, we'll move up to North Carolina. We had a real bad ice storm and all the roads were completely iced over. I was trying to get to work this particular morning and I was about the only car on the road. There was a bridge that I had to cross and as I approached it, I saw a car off the right side of the road, in a treetop. It was a big tree that was leaning over the river only a few feet above the water and the car had skidded off the road landing in the tree. I stopped in the middle of the road to have a look. A lady was in the car. She rolled down her window and asked if I could help her. I said I would and got out of my truck leaving the lights flashing and the motor running. It was so slick it was all I could do to stand on the ice. I inched my way down to the base of the tree and out to the trunk of the car. I told her to open the door and I would hold her arm and take her to my truck. To my surprise she handed me a bag of groceries and said, "Here, take this first. I've got to have these." I took the bag to the car, which took quite an effort and some time.

When I went back and finally was able to get her out of her car and into my truck, she wanted me to take her to a working phone so she could get a tow truck to retrieve her car. I told her nobody has a working phone or power and that no tow trucks would be available either. I did the best I could; I took her to the police station in Pittsboro and left her there. I kept trying to get to work, but both roads were blocked by other stranded vehicles. I never made it to work but I finally made it back home late in the afternoon.

Talking about storms and bad weather, I had been riding out hurricane weather at home in Jacksonville. For some reason, Estelle had gone on up to Nashville, Georgia to be with her parents earlier in the week, but I had both my kids, Lisa and Craig, with me. They were about five and six years old. A lot of the roads were flooded or blocked by falling trees. The only road open that I knew of was a dirt road that ran through a five-mile short cut. I was familiar with the road and had been through it in dry weather many times. It was a very narrow road but in dry weather, you could get over enough to pass a car going in the other direction. We had gone almost the entire distance when I saw a place where the road was washed through. Water had washed out a place about twelve feet wide four feet deep. Now there's no possibility of turning around, backing out, or getting any help. I got out, assessed the situation and found my only option was to jump it. I backed up as far as I safely could, got a good running start and went over it and didn't slow down until I reached the paved surface.

Since we're on the topic bad weather, I was working Microwave Radio for AT&T, feeling sorry for myself having to be out in such bad weather. I was cutting through a road going to Hilliard Microwave Tower to do some work there. My route took me across the Saint Mary River. As I approached the river, I saw a Southern Bell Truck parked on the right side of the road. About half way across the river there was a worker's tent hanging on the telephone cable with a worker inside it working on a trouble. I started counting my blessings. I had never really realized how good I had it

MAKING IT IN CHATHAM

The coldest winter in years was upon us with temperatures below zero and my family was still living in the travel trailer. The water lines that I had buried just under the ground had been frozen for weeks. I had a real need to get my house finished enough to move in. We had a new manager in charge of ESS and I put in a request for a transfer closer to home. There were lots of new ESS machines being installed at that time, so it should not have been a problem. The new ESS manager didn't see it that way and I received word back that I was needed right where I was.

I asked for a short leave of absence so I could get my house livable. According to the rules, you could get a leave of up to a year for hardship cases. She said that this didn't fall in that category and I would have to remain where I was. That Friday, on the way home from Wilmington, I stopped by Heins Telephone Company in Sanford. I found out that they were looking for someone with microwave radio experience and they offered me as job. I told them I needed to give a two-week notice to Southern Bell but that I would come to work then.

When I returned to work on Monday, I turned in my letter of resignation. My immediate boss told me not to resign; maybe he could get me the leave after all. He asked me to sign a leave of absence form and he would fill it out for me. I did that and went to work at Heins Telephone Company. Although the money wasn't quite as good, it was a very good company to work for and close to home. I never did get that leave of absence.

I remember one time I needed a part to repair the microwave radio. One of the engineers, Joe Tucker was also a pilot and had an airplane. We got permission to fly up to the factory and pick up the needed part. I had the Radio back up and running the same day that it had failed. It was wonderful not to have all the red tape that I had been accustomed to.

Almost a year after I left Southern Bell to work for Heins, I got a call from AT&T. They wanted to meet with me about a transfer to the Chatham office near Pittsboro, NC. After a lot of soul searching, I decided to return to AT&T. From my house the best way to go to the nearest store that would have what you needed, was to take Plank Road from highway 42 to Gulf. J.R. Moore's Store had a little of everything so I went there often. From Highway 42 Plank Road was fairly straight for about a quarter mile then had a curve to the left. On Saturdays just beyond the curve was a gathering place for our black brothers. They would park all their cars along Plank Road with about four feet sticking out in the road. Usually there would be fifteen to twenty-five cars parked like this.

One of my friends Paul Craig was moving a D-8 Caterpillar to a new job with a lowboy trailer. With the blade angled it still stuck out about four feet beyond the trailer. About the time Paul came up on the parked cars, a log truck came around the curve headed the other direction. He moved over as far as he could, but Paul had no place to go, and with a load that heavy you're not going to stop. The dozer blade was just the right height to make convertibles out of all those cars, and he did! Neither truck driver was issued a citation but there was a half mile of no parking signs installed along the road.

On a more leisurely thought - I would go fishing once in a while in a local pond. I had a favorite place to dig earthworms, and when I'd get what I wanted, I would hang my potato rake up in a little tree and leave it there until the next time I could go fishing.

When I finally arrived at the Chatham office, drove up in a like new Cadillac, I think it really offended the entire office. A very wealthy friend of mine bought a new Cadillac every year for himself, his wife, and his daughter. His daughter's Cadillac had almost no miles on it and it was offered to me at a very good price. I bought it, my first and only Cadillac.

I couldn't get into the main building until my security clearance was updated. They had a little guard shack building at the main gate they called Chatham Two Office. This is where I was assigned to stay, study, and do odd jobs they wanted done. The road coming in to the office was one mile long and AT&T owned and maintained it. I was told to wear some old clothes the next day that it wouldn't matter if I got paint on them.

I was given ten gallons of gray paint and two gallons each of white and yellow. I was also given a three-inch paintbrush... I was told they wanted me to paint the traffic island where the road turned off the highway. I knew this was just busy work and they wanted to keep me out of their hair for a while. I put in a long handle and three paint rollers and pans from home, and the next day after I checked in, I drove my car down to the traffic island. I painted the entire island washed my rollers and cleaned up the mess and put it all back in my trunk. Then I drove back to Chatham Two with what was left of the paint and the three-inch paint brush. I was washing it when one of the bosses came out to check on me. I told him that I had finished the job. Of course, he didn't believe me, so he wanted to check it out. We got in his truck and drove to the end of the road and he was amazed, he couldn't believe it. He couldn't even find a flaw.

When I finally did get my clearance to gain access to the main building, I was taken down to one of the maintenance rooms and given some radio power supplies to repair. When we took a lunch break, I had the first one working. I gave it to them to put back on the shelf of good spares. That afternoon I repaired another one and gave that to them. Now what I didn't know was that they had six spares and they were all bad. No one had ever been able to repair any of them. The next day I repaired two more. Then one of my nemesis appeared, Butch Jarman brought one of them back and said it had quit working. I was already working on another one and had just gotten it to work. I left it on the workbench and went to take a break. When I returned, it no longer worked either. After looking for a while, I found that someone had pried a vacuum tube out of its socket. I knew this didn't happen on its own. Someone had cut a wire in the chassis of the other unit they brought back. I knew Butch was the saboteur. I caught him alone later and collared him and said, "If you mess with anything I'm working on again I'm going to stomp you're ass." I think I made my point.

After a few years of proving myself technically, I became qualified on all the jobs in the office. Annually we would get an appraisal by the staff and you would receive a ranking of your technical ability. I was always ranked pretty high, but Butch was always ranked number one. He was known in the office as a pipeline. Anything that was said would be passed along to the bosses. Anytime you saw this one particular boss coming around a corner, you knew Butch was right behind him. This gained him the title of a Brown Noser.

One time one of my friends was scheduled to work from Tuesday through Saturday. On Sunday, he was called in on a trouble and worked all day Sunday and Monday. On Thursday afternoon when he was getting off work, his boss told him not to come in Friday or Saturday because he already had his forty hours that week. All AT&T technicians worked under CWA Union contract, which stated that the work schedule must be posted by three PM Thursday of the previous week and cannot be changed after that. This was a clear violation of the contract and I told him they couldn't do that. I told him he should contact his local union steward. The nearest steward was in Charlotte, NC and did not have clearance to get into our office. We didn't have enough members in our office to have our own steward. We held an election and I became the Union Steward. I had a meeting with the bosses and told them they would have to pay him for Friday and Saturday because Sunday and Monday were overtime days. They fought me tooth and nail, but I took it to arbitration and won.

This really put me on their list. They begin calling meetings and I would be forced to defend one of my men. I would have no idea what the meeting was about. They would have three or four bosses attacking me at once, which put me at a distinct disadvantage. One of my men went into an area where he cleaned and did maintenance once a month. There were two doors from different areas; neither could be opened from the inside. He would block the door open while he did his work, but this day he let it slip and locked himself in. Not knowing anything else to do he lit a cigarette and set off the smoke alarm. All of the building was evacuated until the zone alarm could be cleared. They soon found him and all was well until they called a meeting with and wanted to fire him for the incident.

After a hard fought battle, he kept his job. I thought he was pretty smart to know what to do to call attention to his location. Soon I learned that two could play that same game. I could also call meetings. I would do my research and get the facts together. I had taken a few courses at Jacksonville University. One of them was National Labor Relations Law. This gave me an edge in that, so I could nail there hides to the wall. I was working one weekend and had a trouble in my office. In order to clear it I had to climb up in the cable racks to find a short on the circuit. While following the cable I found where someone had tapped into all outgoing phone lines. I followed this and it went to Dodson's office. It came down behind a curtain on his wall, so he would get a light and could monitor all outgoing calls. I cut the splice that was causing my trouble and put a little sticker on it that said "Don't Bug Me". I didn't keep the trouble ticket, so by the time they figured out that one of their monitors wasn't working they wouldn't know who did it. I wired a new circuit to a blank pair of jacks on the patch bay. Our out dial trunks bypassed the billing equipment so there was no record of the calls. I would make a temporary patch that bypassed our office when I made a call so they could not monitor it. I would see my boss peaking around the corner and see that I was on the phone then run back to monitor the call. By the time he returned, I would hang up and pull the patch down. This really upset him. He slipped up on me one time and saw me pulling the patch down and said, "Don't you pull down that patch when I walk up."

I said, "Wait a moment, I reserve the right to terminate any call that I make when I'm finished." Then I asked, "Are you monitoring my calls?" He didn't answer.

There were several offices involved in our project, and Dodson was in charge of all of them. I had just finished working a trouble with Charlie at Hagerstown, MD and he asked, "How's Big Daddy?" That was what they called Dodson.

I said, "He's fine, but if you miss him I'll send him to you."

He laughed and said, "You wish."

I said, "No, I'll really send him if you miss him!" About the time, I disconnected the phone Butch came around the corner. I was still laughing and he asked me what was so funny. I said someone threw a cigarette in the trashcan at Hagerstown and they're having to purge the building. From my workstation, I could view the monitors from many cameras. I knew Butch would get the word to Dodson. It wasn't very long until I saw Dodson leaving in his car, and he was in a big hurry. It was still early in the morning so he had plenty of time. I called Charlie back and said, "Big Daddy's on his way." He raked the entire office over the coals, but finally found nothing had happened at Hagerstown.

A couple of weeks later I meet him in the hall. He said, "You got me last week didn't you?"

I said, "I don't know what you're talking about."

He said, "You know what I'm talking about, you got me!"

Chatham had one outside microwave tower that they maintained at Duncan. I was invited to go with the supervisor and two other technicians to see how it was done.

Of all the towers I had ever seen, this was the smallest, only two channels. One working channel and a patching spare. They got out the book and one would read a step and the other would do it with the supervisor looking over their shoulder. It was all I could do to keep from laughing. It took the best part of the day for them to do what I could have done from memory in fifteen minutes. I just took it all in and they thought they were teaching me the way it was done. At least it got me out of the office for the day.

I was getting my annual appraisal one day from Al Smith and he advised me that I should try to get in a little earlier. I quipped anybody can get in thirty or forty minutes early but it takes real skill to get here right on time. This really got him upset and he said I had been late too many times. I told him I didn't remember being late that often. He went out and got the guards logbook to prove his point. It showed that I was logged in one minute late twice and three minutes late one other time. He said this was entirely unacceptable and I needed to get it off my record. I said I didn't want it off my record because I wanted it to show just how chicken shit AT&T. could really be. He was infuriated at this and said, "I'll tell you one damn thing, you come in late one more time and I'm sending your ass home." We left it at that and went on about our business.

A few months passed but let me mention here that according to the National Labor Relations Law, you are at work when you reach the first controlled entrance. When you're driving up the road, a hydraulic barrier must be lowered before you get to the first guard gate which gets you into the parking lot. Then you walk up to a turnstile where you're on camera again. This time someone inside the building must recognize you and push a button to let you in. This allows you to walk down between the ADT fence to another guard shack. When you get to him, you give him your ID badge and he gives you another one. You are still on camera and he will push and hold a button after the people inside the building have recognized you. They push a button also and the first blast door which weighs tons will slowly motor open, then slowly close behind you, and then the second blast door will open.

Several months passed but one morning I had a flat tire on the way to work and got there about one minute late. Al Smith had been waiting for months for this opportunity. He made me wait for three or four minutes at each gate before opening it. By the time, the second blast door opened for me to get in the building he and Al Holt were standing there to greet me. He looked menacingly at his watch and said, "Me and you talked about this didn't we?" I said yes. "Well you know what to expect," and he sent me home."

I left and went to my Recording Studio in Sanford because I had a good bit of work I could do there. I worked there long hours for the next three days. I didn't answer the phone or anything, I just worked on orders that I had. It was time for some of my customers to pick up their orders so I answered the phone about ten o'clock that morning. It was Al Smith on the phone and he asked me why I wasn't at work. I said, "Al, you sent me home, remember?"

He said, "I just sent you home for one day."

I said, "You didn't say that; you just sent me home and I had a lot of work I needed to do here."

"Well come in tomorrow."

I said, "OK, I will." When I got back to work, I found out that they had a major TD – 2 Radio trouble and no one had been able to fix it. The radio had failed shortly after I had been sent home and it had all come down around Al's neck. I had the radio repaired in about forty-five minutes. The next day I was called into the office to be reprimanded for not being at work for the extra days.

Al Holt and Al Smith were telling their versions of what transpired. Al Smith said I just sent him home for one day, and to my surprise Al Holt said, no you didn't say that, you just sent him home.

With that, the session was closed with a little egg on Al's face.

One time we had a twelve-inch water line that started leaking and to stop the leak, I got our welding machine. It was a nice AC/DC machine capable of five hundred amps. I set the machine on reverse polarity and 250 amps and was able to weld up the leak while still under pressure. This impressed the Big Boss and he thought we should have more people qualified to weld. He decided that I should teach a welding class.

We had scrap metal that we were removing and they wanted a trailer to haul sand for the road as well. The first thing I built was a trailer for that purpose. Then we built some tables. One of the night shift guys saw the tables we were building and said he wanted one too. I put a big hand written sign on a pile of scrap metal that said, *table kit for Bill Griffin, some assembly required.*

After I had taught basic welding to the class, Dodson thought that we should go and get certified. I told him that it was not that easy to become a certified welder and the test was much harder than the basic welding we had done. Never the less he sent us anyway. The outcome was as I predicted, no one passed. You had to weld two pieces of five-inch high-pressure steam pipe end to end and grind them down so they looked like one pipe. Then they put it in a hydraulic press and bent it to the shape of a horseshoe. Next, they would examine it and x-ray it. If any flaws were present, you failed the test. The test was administered by Combustion Engineering Company. You also had to know a little about metallurgy and be able to select the correct welding rods for each job. This was far beyond the scope of our class. Nevertheless, we at least had a few people capable of basic welding.

We had a new guy that they had hired, Charlie Graham. Charlie was assigned to me so I could teach him radio. Charlie had just gotten out of the Navy and he was very sharp in electronics. We soon became close friends. Once a month I would go to Charlotte to attend a Union Meeting and I was allowed to take someone with me.

This one particular trip I took Charlie with me. I always got in to Charlotte a little early so I could talk to the guys from the other offices and discuss their problems. The guys in the Charlotte office played chess on their breaks and other time off and I was one of their only visitors who played any chess. They always wanted to play me. I wasn't a great player, but I could hold my own with them. I was in the middle of one of these games and got called away to some business, so I asked Charlie if he played chess. He said a little bit, so I asked him to take over for me. I was away about thirty minutes and when I came back, Charlie was playing two games at the same time, and won both. On the way back to Chatham, I asked Charlie how he learned to play chess so well. He told me that he was a member of a national chess club, and was nationally ranked sixth. I'm thinking *no wonder.*

One Saturday I was going to replace the roof on my Studio, and asked Charlie if he would come over and help. I had a couple of other guys to help also, He said, "If you'll furnish the beer I'll be there." I asked him what brand he wanted, and he told me. I said I'd have a good supply for him.

Charlie came over and we were already on the roof. He went to the cooler to check out the beer, took out a can and looked it over. Then he said, "What is this?"

I asked, "What's wrong? That's the right kind isn't it?"

"Yes, but these little cans are the training size; I wanted the large magnum size."

Another time I had a problem with one of my half-track recorders, an Ampex ATR 800. This recorder uses a chase lock loop to keep it in time. A light shines through a fan and the pulses are refined into square waves and counted so the machine can locate a particular place on the tape. It also uses the pulses to keep the run speed constant. It would locate OK, but when running constant speed it was jittering. During normal operation, it should slew the pulse forward if it's running slow or retard the pulse if it's running too fast.

My first thought was to replace the motor, but I found out that it would cost over eight hundred dollars, so I thought maybe I should prove it wasn't something else first. I could see the pulse on the scope and it was jumping all the time. Trouble shooting this circuit can be a nightmare because it's a big circle. Is the jitter because of the circuit not working properly or is it the fault of the motor? I asked Charlie if he would come down and give me a hand; maybe two heads are better than one. He said that audio stuff is nothing but I'll come down and help you. When he arrived, I gave him the book that contained the circuit description. After reading it for about thirty minutes he said, "This is a complicated son of a bitch."

I said, "It's just audio Charlie." We didn't manage to fix it, however. After a lot's of research, I found the reputed guru for Ampex Recorders in Atlanta, Georgia. After talking to him and relaying my problem to him, he wanted me to send it to him. I sent it to him and he kept it for a month or so, but was unable to get it to work right either. When I got it back, I decided to bite the bullet and ordered the new motor.

It was tough to install but when I did, it worked perfectly. Sometimes first impressions are the best.

Charlie was from Maryland and he had a chance to go to work near where he was from but he was unsure of his ability to work on the types of radio that the job would require. I had worked on those before so I told him how they worked and assured him that he would have no trouble. He went up and got the job. Our office decided to give Charlie a going away party. Charlie was well liked by almost everyone in the office and he could get away with just about anything. He came the day of the party and had with him a little spray bottle which he had labeled "Ugly Repellant, Clerk Strength" and gave it to our clerks, Pat and Mary. They laughed it off. Only Charlie could have gotten away with that.

That night after a dinner, Charlie gave a good speech and told everyone how much he had enjoyed working with them. He had finished talking and started to walk away; then he turned back and said, "Oh! There's one more thing I'd like to say. Butch Jarman is not qualified to carry Bill Tripp's toolbox." I felt like crawling under the table. Butch was one of the few who chose not to attend the dinner. Butch had been sent to Kansas City to teach a six-week technical school and Charlie was sent to the school. I knew a lot of the guys that were sent to the school. When the school is finished, the class writes an appraisal of the instructors. The school was almost complete and I was talking with Charlie on the phone one night. He said, "You just wait until I write him up.

That dumb SOB don't know a damn thing about what he's teaching."

I said, "No, no, Charlie; think about it. We don't want him to come back to our office. You guys need to make him walk on water then you can let the next class tell it like it is. Once he takes the job, he will lose his security clearance then he can't come back here. So, Charlie talked it up with his classmates and I made all the calls I could to support the cause and they did it. He took the job permanently, sold his house and moved to Kansas City. This gave him a little reprieve before his next class. He taught two classes then was assigned a desk job, which he hated. And that is how I finally got rid of my nemesis.

AT&T was offering some early outs for people who might want to retire early. They would pay you a lump sum upon retirement. You would sign up but they would select the exact date of retirement any time within one year. On the surface, this sounds good but they have plans that you would never think that they would sink so low. They made the retirement date at the end of the year so everything you made that year plus your bonus put you in a higher tax bracket. About forty percent of your bonus was taken for tax.

Your retirement was figured on the number of years completed. They retired me one day before my twenty-seventh year was completed so that it didn't count for my retirement. That chapter of my life is now closed. We never got the insurance coverage or the class A telephone for life that was promised when we were hired. AT&T was broken up and transferred, reorganized, renamed and played like a shell game so you could no longer find where to go for help. I gave up and quit trying.

MY MOORE COUNTY STORIES

I was happily running my studio in Sanford when a friend called and asked if I would mind coming to Moore County to help him set up a commercial TV station. It was just a little low power station but I got it up and running. That led to a request to help set one at Sandhills Community College.

Then later I was asked to work for Moore County School System. Some of the schools had their own TV Studio programs. They were broadcast in house on cable. Without going into a lot of the details this led to a full time job offer from Moore County Schools. I took the job and wound up working there for seven years.

While there, I took care of everything from intercom, PA systems, overhead projectors, VCRs, and laminating machines. The job encompassed every school in the county. That was quite a job for one person. I still ran my studio in Sanford at the same time. The technology was not yet available to burn CDs so it was all on VCRs. They had training videos that they wanted converted from English to Spanish, so I rigged up a little studio in my office. I could separate the video from the audio then display the English on a screen and a translator would read it in Spanish. This involved my borrowing equipment from my studio to be able to do this.

I had one of the very first high quality color printers, a Raster Ops unit that cost twelve thousand dollars. The main problem with this unit was that it required special paper and the cost of the paper made it impractical to print large projects. The finished copy was beautiful and with the available software, the picture could be manipulated to add or remove portions. I used this to make projects for Moore County Schools. I never charged them anything. I took my studio microphones and set up sound systems for them to use for special events.

One time we had groundbreaking ceremonies for two new schools and the Secretary of Education and the Governor of the state flew in by helicopter to give their speeches. There was no AC power available at these locations so I got one of my DC Amplifiers that I had mounted in a box containing a motorcycle battery. This could be plugged into a cigarette lighter and charged or I also had a small battery charger that could be charged with AC. I also borrowed a mixer and speakers. This did the job very well. Everyone got to speak and I recharged the unit between locations with the cigarette lighter.

There were many other times that I loaned my equipment to the School System with nothing in return. In the basement of the building that my office was in were thousands of books. A lot of these books were new samples that were sent for the schools to review and maybe adopt to use in the classrooms. Some of them were books that were used for a couple of years then replaced. The Literature and Math books changed very little and could be used. They had decided to haul them to the landfill. They had already loaded out three tractor trailer truck loads of books when I thought of one of my neighbors that was home schooling his kids and asked if I might take a few books for him. They said, "Absolutely not!" They didn't want to help anyone doing home schooling. They hauled them all to the landfill.

On another occasion, someone from Pinehurst donated a complete collection of National Geographic Magazines from the very first edition up until the present time to Pinecrest High School. They were in perfect condition and arranged in sequence. What a wonderful resource. Instead of these being recognized for what they were, they were put on a big table and people were told to take any that they wanted. The early aviation, World War I, and World War II were quickly taken. The ones that remained after two weeks were thrown away. That was when I changed my mind about doing all the things I had been doing for free.

I did make a few books for some of the people that worked there. I had a Channel Bind System that would put a hardbound cover on a book. I had to buy the covers from Channel Bind and pay for the printing on the covers, but it looked very professional. The highway department was finalizing the purchase of the land for the 421 bypass around Sanford and my studio and some other property that I owned were in the right of way. We couldn't agree on a price that I felt was fair. They gave me an ultimatum. "We have deposited a check at the court house and you have six weeks to vacate the premises." They gave me nowhere near enough money to replace what I had there. My ace in the hole, however was that they had to move and rewire my studio equipment.

They were under the delusion that any electrician could rewire a studio. I gave them bids that I had gotten from some studio wiring companies in Nashville, Tennessee. They were still unable to find any one company that would do the entire job. I offered to do it myself for the lowest bid. They accepted this offer and they agreed to give me drafts to cover my expenses as I progressed. I decided that I would be better off taking my retirement from the school system and doing this work myself. So I retired and for the next two years built and wired my new studio on farmland that I already had. I do a little studio work there and work with my blueberries. I feed the fish in my ponds, write a few songs and books, but mostly I just lay low and play my guitar.

NEW SONGS

STREETS OF NASHVILLE

I WALKED THE STREETS OF NASHVILLE, WITH MY HAND FULL OF SONGS
I THOUGHT SOMEDAY MY BREAK MIGHT COME, SO I KEPT MOVING ON
BUT MY CHANCES WERE MIGHTY THIN, AND DEFEAT DRAGGED ME DOWN
WHEN YOU WALK THE STREETS OF NASHVILLE, YOU'RE GOING ROUND AND
    ROUND

I SANG MY SONGS, A THOUSAND TIMES, AND I THOUGHT I HAD IT RIGHT
I PLAYED AT SOME OLD BAR IN TOWN, TILL TWO OR THREE, EACH NIGHT
THEN I PACKED UP, MY OLD GUITAR, AND HEADED, OUT OF TOWN
AND LEFT THE STREETS OF NASHVILLE, GOING ROUND, AND ROUND

CHORUS:

    YOU WALK THE STREETS OF NASHVILLE, OH! YOU COUNTRY FOOL
    DON'T YOU KNOW, THAT THERE'S A THOUSAND THERE, JUST AS GOOD
        AS YOU
    AND THERE'S NO PLACE FOR, A COUNTRY BOY, IN THAT COUNTRY
        TOWN
    WHEN YOU WALK THE STREETS OF NASHVILLE, YOU'RE GOING ROUND
        AND ROUND

REPEAT CHORUS:

THE ROAD TO DEMASCUS

A HEART FILLED WITH HATE AND CURSING AS HE STARTED ON HIS WAY
CHRISTIANS WERE THE QUARRY THEY WOULD SURELY HAVE TO PAY
HE WOULD PERSECUTE RELENTLESSLY THAT'S WHAT HIS ORDERS SAY
BUT THE ROAD TO DEMASCUS WOULD CHANGE HIM ON THAT DAY

CHORUS:
    THE ROAD TO DEMASCUS, THE ROAD TO DEMASCUS
    THE MIND OF SAUL, WAS CHANGED, ON THAT DAY
    THE ROAD TO DEMASCUS, THE ROAD TO DEMASCUS
    THAT'S WHERE JESUS SHOWED HIM THE RIGHT WAY

A BRIGHT LIGHT SHONE UPON HIM, AND HE FELL UPON THE GROUND
THE OTHERS WITH HIM SAW IT, BUT THEY NEVER HEARD A SOUND
A VOICE ASKED HIM SO PLAINLY, WHY PERSECUTEST, THOU ME
THEN HE WAS BLINDED FOR THREE DAYS, SO LATER HE MIGHT SEE

REPEAT CHORUS:

FOR THREE DAYS HE WAS LED ABOUT, AND STILL HE COULD NOT SEE
THEN GOD TOLD ANANIAS, HE'S A CHOSEN VESSEL TO ME
GO FIND AND SAY UNTO HIM, THE LORD GOD HAS SENT ME
SO YOU'LL BE FILLED WITH THE HOLY GHOST, AND ONCE AGAIN YOU'LL SEE

REPEAT CHORUS:

TAG:

SHAMROCK CAFE

SHE WAS MY WAITRESS, THE DAY I CAME IN
SHARING A LUNCH BREAK, WITH SOME OF MY FRIENDS
THE SMILE ON HER FACE, STOLE MY HEART AWAY
DOWN AT, THE SHAMROCK CAFE

CHORUS:

> YES THE GIRL AT THE SHAMROCK, CAUGHT ME WITH HER SMILE
> WE MET FELL IN LOVE, THEN DATED A WHILE
> I ASK HER TO MARRY, AND SHE SAID OK
> DOWN AT THE SHAMROCK CAFE

TIME PASSED SO QUICKLY, AND SOON THERE WERE THREE
THE GIRL FROM THE SHAMROCK, THE BABY AND ME
I'LL NEVER FORGET, HOW WE MET ON THAT DAY
DOWN AT THE SHAMROCK CAFE

CHORUS:

Shamrock Care, Wildwood Crest, NJ

SING ME A STORY

ONE NIGHT IN A BAR ROOM, WHILE OUT ON A RAMBLE
I PICKED UP MY GUITAR AND TOLD WHERE I'D BEEN
THE BIGGEST MAN IN THE BAR ROOM, LOOKED AT ME SQUARELY
AND SAID I THINK THAT'S A LIE! BUT WOULD YOU SING IT AGAIN

CHORUS:

> SING ME A SONG, THAT TELLS ME A STORY
> IT MAY BE THE TRUTH, OR IT MAY BE ALL LIES
> SING ME A SONG, SING SO SINCERELY
> AND IF IT'S A SAD ONE, PUT TEARS IN OUR EYES

THEN I TOLD HIM A STORY, OF A BEAUTIFUL LADY
WHO ONCE FELL IN LOVE WITH, A HANDSOME YOUNG MAN
THEN HE HAD TO LEAVE, AND SHE YEARNED FOR HIM DAILY
WHY DID HE GO, SHE COULD NOT UNDERSTAND

REPEAT CHORUS:

HE SAID THAT'S MY STORY, AND IT HAPPENED JUST LIKE THAT!
SHE WAS MY SWEETHEART, AND THEY TOOK ME AWAY
THE KANGAROO COURT SAID THAT I OWED THEM TAXES
THEY PUT ME IN PRISON, FOR TEN YEARS AND A DAY

REPEAT CHORUS:

THIS OLD COWBOY

I USE TO BE A COWBOY, I USE TO ROPE AND RIDE
I USE TO WEAR A STETSON HAT, SIX GUN BY MY SIDE
I SPENT A LOT OF STARRY NIGHTS, OUT ON THE LONESOME TRAIL
I'VE EVEN SPENT A NIGHT OR TWO, LOCKED IN THE COUNTY JAIL

I'VE TRAVELED LOTS OF PLACES, BUT I NEVER SETTLED DOWN
I MET A LOVELY LADY, SHE WANTED ME AROUND
SHE SAID SHE REALLY LOVED ME, I GUESS I LOVED HER TOO
BUT I STILL HAD RAMBLING FEVER, JUST TO MUCH LEFT TO DO

CHORUS:

NOW THERE'S DUST ON THE SADDLE, THAT'S CARRIED ME SO FAR
AND THERE'S RUST ON THE STRINGS, OF MY OLD FLAT TOP GUITAR
I SEEM TO BE THE VERY LAST, OF A DYING BREED OF MEN
THIS OLD COWBOY WILL SOON BE GONE, HE WONT BE BACK AGAIN

INSTRUMENTAL BRAKE:

I PUT OLD PAINT TO PASTURE, HIS LEGS WERE TIRED AND SORE
FOR MANY YEARS WE'D ROAMED THE TRAILS, IN SEARCH OF SOMETHING
MORE
THE ONE TRUE LOVE I FOUND IN LIFE, I LET HER GET AWAY
NOW I'LL WISH I COULD, GO BACK IN TIME, UNTIL MY DYING DAY

REPEAT CHORUS:

INSTRUMENTAL BRAKE:

REPEAT CHORUS:

TELL ME THE STORY OF JESUS

WHEN I GOT TO THE CHURCH SUNDAY MORNING
I SAT DOWN IN THE VERY LAST PEW
A STRANGER CAME AND SAT THERE BESIDE ME
AND ASK WHAT THE PREACHER WILL DO

WORRIED BY HIS SINFUL CONDITION
SO RESTLESS, ALL THE NIGHT LONG
HE NEEDED GRACE, LOVE, FAITH, AND REDEMPTION
AND A SOUL MOVING GOSPEL SONG

WILL HE TELL ME THE STORY OF JESUS?
HOW HE CAME DOWN FROM HEAVEN ABOVE
WILL HE TELL ME THE STORY OF JESUS?
ABOUT GRACE, COMPASSION AND LOVE

INSTRUMENTAL BRAKE:

I TOLD HIM ABOUT OUR NEW PREACHER
I THINK THAT YOU WILL BE BLESSED
HE GIVES A MIGHTY GOOD SERMON
SO GOOD FOR THOSE WHO ARE STRESSED

WILL THE WORDS COME STRAIGHT FROM THE BIBLE?
HE ASKED, WITH TEARS IN HIS EYES
IF THE WORDS DON'T COME FROM THE BIBLE
THERE'S A CHANCE THAT, THEY MAY CONTAIN LIES

WILL HE TELL ME THE STORY OF JESUS?
ABOUT FORGIVENESS AND LOVE ONCE AGAIN
WILL HE TELL ME THE STORY OF JESUS?
HOW HE DIED ON THE CROSS FOR OUR SINS

WILL HE TELL ME THE STORY OF JESUS?
HOW, BY GRACE THROUGH FAITH YOU'RE SAVED
BELIEVING YOU WILL BE FORGIVEN
AND THROUGH JESUS BE SPARED FROM THE GRAVE

TAG:

A WANTED MAN

WHILE WALKING THRU THE STREETS
OF A LONESOME OLD TOWN
I LISTEN TO THE RAINDROPS
AS THEY BEAT UPON THE GROUND
NOBODY CARES ABOUT ME
I GUESS THAT IT'S MY FAULT
BUT IF I DON'T KEEP ON MOVING
I KNOW THAT I'LL GET CAUGHT

CHORUS:

    CAUSE I'M A WANTED MAN, WANTED MAN
    YOU MAKE NO FUTURE PLANS
    YOU'RE ALWAYS IN A RACE
    TO WHERE NO ONE KNOWS YOUR FACE
    WHEN YOU'RE A WANTED MAN

MY FRIENDS ALL TRIED TO CHANGE ME
BUT I GUESS IT'S JUST MY WAY
I WOULDN'T LISTEN TO NOBODY
I THOUGHT THAT CRIME COULD PAY
I SHOT A MAN FOR MONEY
WAY DOWN IN TENNESSEE
NOW THE SHERIFF AND HIS POSSE
ARE LOOKING FOR ME

REPEAT CHORUS:

I SPENT A RESTLESS NIGHT
IN AN OLD DESERTED HOME
I SAW THEM CLOSING IN ON ME
ABOUT THE BREAK OF DAWN

LIFE'S ADVENTURE – FROM THEN TILL WHEN

WITH NO CHANCE OF ESCAPING
THE LAW MEN ALL AROUND
IF I TRY TO RUN I KNOW
THEY'RE GONE TO GUN ME DOWN

REPEAT CHORUS:

WELL I'M A WANTED MAN
WANTED MAN, I'M A WANTED MAN

THINK IT OVER

BEFORE YOU START TO PLAY AROUND, THINK IT OVER
THINK OF ALL THE HURT, A BROKEN HOME CAN BRING
AND IF YOU STILL, BELIEVE ITS WORTH, THE PAIN AND SORROW
THEN WHAT'S RIGHT AND WRONG TO YOU, DON'T MEAN A THING

WILL THE CHILDREN UNDERSTAND, YOUR WAY OF THINKING
WHEN YOU TAKE AWAY, THEIR MOTHER, OR THEIR DAD
CAN YOU EVER FIND THE LOVE, THAT YOU'VE BEEN WANTING
WHEN YOU KNOW YOU'VE HURT A FAMILY SO BAD

CHORUS:

    THINK IT OVER, BEFORE YOU START TO BREAK A HEART INTO
    SHOULD LITTLE HEARTS BE BROKEN, HEARTS THAT ARE SO TRUE
    THEY'LL NEVER HAVE ANOTHER HOME, WITH A REAL MOM AND DAD
    SO THINK IT OVER, BEFORE THINGS GET THIS BAD

INSTRUMENTAL BRAKE

MOD UP 1

REPEAT CHORUS:

NEITHER ONE'S RED ANYMORE

IN YOUR LETTERS YOU WROTE OF THE LOVE IN YOUR HEART
AND RED ROSES I SENT TO YOUR DOOR
NOW THE NOTES MAKE ME CRY
AND THE PEDALS ARE DRY
AND NEITHER ONE'S RED ANYMORE

CHORUS:

    WHEN HE CAME ALONG
    SOON OUR LOVE WAS GONE
    THEN, YOU JUST WALKED OUT THE DOOR
    NOW THE PEDALS HAVE DRIED
    AND THE NOTES, MAKE ME CRY
    AND NEITHER ONE'S RED ANYMORE

 INSTRUMENTAL BREAK:

YOU ALWAYS WOULD SEND, LOVE LETTERS BACK THEN
WHICH I ALWAYS READ ORE AND ORE
A BOUQUET, EACH DAY
AS I PASSED YOUR WAY
NOW NEITHER ONE'S READ ANYMORE

REPEAT CHORUS:

INSTRUMENTAL BREAK:

REPEAT CHORUS:

TAG:

SUPPORTING THAT WELFARE

WE'VE GOT LOTS OF FOLKS ON WELFARE, AND SOME DESERVE TO BE
BUT MOST OF THEM, CAN DO A JOB, AS WELL AS YOU AND ME
BUT THEY'LL SET BACK IN, THAT EASY CHAIR AND NOT HIT A LICK ALL DAY
THEY'RE NOT GOING TO WORK NONE, NO! CAUSE UNCLE SAM HANDS OUT
    THEIR PAY

CHORUS:

    THEY'RE ON WELFARE, DRAW THAT ROCKING CHAIR
    I WORK HARD EVERY DAY, BUT UNCLE SAM TAKES ALL MY PAY

INSTRUMENTAL:

NOW YOU MAY THINK I'M BITTER, I GUESS I SOUND THAT WAY
BUT IT DANG SURE GETS ME ALL RILED UP, EACH TIME I DRAW MY PAY
AND I SEE THE HUNK, THAT SAMS DONE TOOK, AND THE LITTLE THAT I'VE
    GOT LEFT
THEN I WATCH HIM GIVE IT ALL AWAY, WHILE ME, I STARVE TO DEATH

CHORUS:

    I'M SUPPORTING THAT WELFARE, THAT OLD ROCKING CHAIR
    I WORK HARD EVERY DAY, BUT UNCLE SAM TAKES ALL MY PAY

INSTRUMENTAL:

NOW I'VE DONE AND RESEARCHED HISTORY, AND I WENT A LONG WAY
    BACK
AND I CAN'T EVER FIND ONE TIME, WHERE THEY REALLY CUT OUR TAX
THEY'LL TALK ABOUT A BIG TAX CUT, AND MAKE PROMISES GALORE
BUT WHEN THE DUST HAS SETTLED BACK, WE'VE GOT MORE TAX THAN
    BEFORE

CHORUS:

    WE'VE GOT A LITTLE MORE WELFARE, THAT OLD ROCKING CHAIR
    I WORK HARD EVERY DAY, BUT UNCLE SAM TAKES ALL MY PAY

AD LIB

YEAH AND I'M GETTING TIRED OF IT TO
JUST TAKING ALL MY HARD EARNED MONEY
THEN JUST GIVING IT AWAY, I CAN'T STAND THIS

I'M GONNA RISE

WHEN THE GOOD LORD CALLS MY NAME, I'M GONNA RISE
WHEN HE GATHERS ALL HIS SAINTS, I'M GONNA RISE
OLE SATAN TOLD A LIE, HE'LL REGRET THAT BYE AND BYE
WHEN THE GOOD LORD CALLS MY NAME I'M GONNA RISE

CHORUS:

>WE WILL RISE UP IN HIS GLORY
>THAT HAS BEEN THE CHRISTIAN STORY
>FOR HE LOVES US, AND HE'LL NEVER, LET US DOWN
>DOWN THE STRAIGHT AND NARROW WAY
>HE WILL GUIDE US EVERYDAY
>AT ITS END'S WHERE, OUR REWARD WILL BE FOUND
>LORD, LORD, AT ITS END IS WHERE OUR REWARD WILL BE FOUND

WHEN OLE SATAN KNOCKS ME DOWN, I'M GONNA RISE
IF I'M FLAT UPON THE GROUND, I'M GONNA RISE
THERE MAY BE MUD UPON MY CLOTHS, BUT I'LL SMELL JUST LIKE A ROSE
MY GOD WILL HELP ME UP, AND I'M GONNA RISE

REPEAT CHORUS:

TAG:

RIVER SWAMP

COON TRACKS ALONG THE RIVER BANK
CLAM SHELLS AND A ROTTEN PLANK
THREE WILD DUCKS SEE ME AND TURN
AND THERE'S A RABBIT ON THE RUN

CHORUS:

>RIVER SWAMP, RIVER SWAMP
>CRAWDAD'S PLACE AND MOCCASINS HAUNT
>MOSQUITOES AND THE GATORS THAT I DON'T WANT
>BUT MY HOMES IN, THE RIVER SWAMP

A BULL FROG JUMPS ALONG THE WAY
TURTLES SUN THERE EVERY DAY
I'VE SEEN THE PANTHER AND THE BEAR
BUT THEY MUST HAVE GONE SOMEWHERE

REPEAT CHORUS:

FISHING IN CLEAR WATER STREAMS
HOOT OWLS HUNTING WHILE I DREAM
THESE ARE THE THINGS THAT I CALL HOME
AND I HOPE THEY'RE NEVER GONE

REPEAT CHORUS:

BACK TO ALABAMA

I LEFT MY HOME IN ALABAM, AND I CROSSED THE DIXON LINE
BUT I TOOK ALONG A MEMORY, OF A GIRL I'D LEFT BEHIND
I DIDN'T KNOW I'D MISS HER SO, BUT I FOUND, I WAS WRONG
AND EVERY DAY I THINK OF HER, AND WISH THAT I WAS HOME

IT COST A LOT TO TRAVEL NOW, AND THE JOB I'VE GOT IS BAD
IT TAKES EVERY CENT TO PAY THE RENT, AND FEED THIS HUNGRY LAD
MY HEART IS SORE AND I MISS HER MORE, EACH DAY AS TIME GOES ON
AND EVERY DAY I THINK OF HER, AND WISH THAT I WAS HOME

CHORUS:

I'M GOING BACK TO ALABAMA, WHERE MY SUNSHINE IS
BACK TO ALABAMA, THAT'S WHERE I WANT TO LIVE
I'M GONNA FIND THAT WOMAN, I'VE BEEN MISSING FOR SO LONG
AND FOREVER MORE, MAKE ALABAM MY HOME

INSTRUMENTAL:

I DRAW MY PAY NEXT SATURDAY, AND IT'S TIME TO PAY MY RENT
BUT EARLY MONDAY MORNING, THEY'LL WONDER WHERE I WENT
THEY'LL FIND A NOTE IN WHICH I WROTE, FOREVER I'LL BE GONE
'CAUSE I'M NOT EVER COMING BACK, 'CAUSE ALABAM'S MY HOME

REPEAT CHORUS:

CANTEENS, COWBOYS AND CROCKS

SPOKEN INTRO:

> BACK WHEN I WAS 9 OR 10, I CAN STILL REMEMBER WHEN
> ON SATURDAY MORNING AT THE MOVIE MATINEE
> THE COWBOY ON THE SILVER SCREEN, WE'D WATCH HIM RIDE ACROSS
>   THE PLANES
> BUT WHEN HIS CANTEEN OF WATER HAD RUN DRY
> HE'D HOLD IT UPSIDE DOWN, THEN TOSS IT TO THE GROUND

I'D SAY NOW THAT'S A CROCK
HE WOULDN'T THROW IT ON THE TRAIL, EACH TIME THAT THE LAST DROP
    FELL
HE'D KEEP IT TILL HE FOUND ANOTHER WELL
AND THEN HE'D STUMBLE INTO TOWN
AND AT THE FIRST SALOON THAT COULD BE FOUND
ORDER BRANDY, TO WASH THE TRAIL DUST DOWN

CHORUS:

> CANTEENS, COWBOYS AND CROCKS
> A CANTEEN, HORSE AND SADDLE, THAT'S EVERYTHING HE'S GOT
> NO! I DIDN'T COUNT HIS SIX GUN, THAT THING MUST COST A LOT
> CANTEENS, COWBOYS AND CROCKS

THEN THERE'S A POSSE, ON THE OUTLAWS TRAIL
GUNS BLAZIN' BUT HE NEVER FELL
TEN SHOTS FROM A SIX GUN AND GIVE A YELL
THEN HE'D THROW THAT GUN AWAY
LIKE YOU COULD FIND ONE ANY DAY
THAT SHOT THAT MANY TIMES, BUT I'D LIKE TO SAY

NOW THAT'S A CROCK

REPEAT CHORUS:

DON'T LET FOREVER
TURN INTO NEVER AGAIN

FOR MANY YEARS I'VE LOVED YOU LADY
AND WE'VE DANCED IN MANY ROOMS
AS OUR BODY'S HAVE AGED
IT'S HARD TO FIND A NIMBLE TUNE
SO TONIGHT HOLD ME CLOSELY
JUST THINK HOW GOOD IT HAS BEEN
AND DON'T LET FOREVER TURN INTO NEVER AGAIN

NOW I KNOW THAT YOUTH IS FLEETING
BUT MY HEART STILL HOLDS YOU TRUE
A GREAT LIFE SPENT TOGETHER
NOW THERE'S SOME THINGS WE CAN'T DO
BUT I'LL ALWAYS REMEMBER
JUST HOW GOOD IT HAS BEEN
AND DON'T LET FOREVER, TURN INTO NEVER AGAIN

CHORUS:

    WHEN YOUR LIFE IS OVER, YOU KNOW GOD HAS PAID THE WAY
    THERE'S A MANSION WAITING FOR YOU IN HEAVEN
    AND THERE'S JUST ONE THING TO SAY
    THANK YOU LORD FOR YOUR MERCY
    AND FOR FORGIVING ALL MY SINS
    I KNOW THAT FOREVER, WONT BE NEVER AGAIN

FIND YOURSELF A ROCK

THERE ARE SOME THINGS, YOU NEED TO KNOW
ABOUT THE STORMS OF LIFE
YOU'LL NEED SOMEONE TO HELP YOU THROUGH
YOUR TROUBLES FEAR AND STRIFE
THEY'LL BE SOME THINGS THAT YOU JUST CAN'T
HANDLE ON YOUR OWN
SO FIND SOMEONE WHO'LL BE RIGHT THERE
AND WON'T LEAVE YOU ALONE

CHORUS:

    FIND YOURSELF A ROCK, NOT A ROLLING STONE
    FIND A FIRM FOUNDATION, TO BUILD YOUR LIFE UPON
    PUT YOUR TRUST IN JESUS, HE'LL KEEP YOU FROM ALL WRONG
    FIND YOURSELF A ROCK, NOT A ROLLING STONE

THE DEVIL WITH HIS WILEY WAY
WILL CATCH YOU IF HE CAN
HE'LL TRY AND MAKE YOU BELIEVE
THAT GOD WONT HOLD YOUR HAND
HE'S ALWAYS BEEN A LIAR
SO DON'T FIGHT HIM ON YOUR OWN
GET YOURSELF A SOLID ROCK
TO FIGHT THAT ROLLING STONE

REPEAT CHORUS:

TAG: JESUS IS THE ROCK, NOT A ROLLING STONE

HUNGRY

CHORUS:

> HUNGRY, HUNGRY, HUNGRY, HUNGRY ALL THE TIME
> NO I'M NOT REALLY HUNGRY, BUT IT OCCUPIES MY MIND

MY HUNGER WAS TELLING ME, TO EAT, AND THERE I SAT
LOOKING DOWN AT MY MIDDLE, COMPLETELY LINED WITH FAT

WHY WOULD MY SYSTEM TRY AND TRICK ME, AND MAKE ME FEED IT MORE
WHEN IF I GET ANY BIGGER, I WONT FIT THROUGH THE DOOR

REPEAT CHORUS:

I CURSE AT IT AND TELL IT, THAT I DON'T CARE A DAMN
YOU'VE GOT YOUR OWN STOREHOUSE, COMPLETELY LINED WITH HAM

DON'T PESTER ME, EAT YOUR OWN, THAT'S WHAT FAT IS FOR
AND NO MATTER HOW MUCH I FEED YOU, YOU ALWAYS WANT SOME MORE

REPEAT CHORUS:

A STOMACH THAT'S OUT OF CONTROL THAT I MUST REPRIMAND
IT'S TIME THAT I LAID DOWN THE LAW, IT'S TIME THAT YOU CAVE IN

NO MORE SNACKING AFTER MEALS, IF I EVEN GIVE THAT MUCH
I'LL PUT YOU TO BED HUNGRY, AND MAYBE SKIP A LUNCH

REPEAT CHORUS:

A LITE NUTRITIOUS BREAKFAST, THAT'S ALL YOUR GONNA GET
UNTIL YOU START TO LOSE THEM POUNDS, AND I HAVEN'T SEEN THAT YET

BUT I'M GLAD WE HAD THIS LITTLE TALK, SO YOU WILL UNDERSTAND
THE REASON FOR ME WALKING ROUND,
A VERY HUNGRY MAN

REPEAT CHORUS:

I KNOW THAT I LOVE YOU

WAY UP IN THE MOUNTAINS, ALL COVERED WITH SNOW
OR EVERGREEN FOREST, WHERE WILD FLOWERS GROW
I KNOW THAT I LOVE YOU, AND I ALWAYS WILL
IN FOGGY BOTTOM, OR ON, MOCKINGBIRD HILL

IN UPPER MANHATTAN, OR DOWN ON THE FARM
IN A SOLID GOLD MANSON, OR A WOODEN, LAP BARN
I KNOW THAT I LOVE YOU, AND I'LL NEVER STOP
IN SOME LONESOME VALLEY, OR ON ROCKY TOP

CHORUS:

    ON A LONG OCEAN VOYAGE, OR A SHIP TO THE MOON
    THE COLD OF DECEMBER, OR THE WARM SUN IN JUNE
    I KNOW THAT I LOVE YOU, WHEREVER YOU ARE
    BE IT RIGHT BY MY SIDE, OR ON SOME DISTANT STAR

INSTRUMENTAL BREAK:

REPEAT CHORUS:

TAG:

    BE IT RIGHT BY MY SIDE, OR ON SOME DISTANT STAR

I'M TRYING TO GET OVER YOU
AND OUR OLD LOVE AFFAIR

I HARDLY EVER HAVE A DATE, OR GO OUT ANYWHERE
THE ONE THAT CAUSED US TO BREAK UP, NOW NO LONGER CARES
I THINK ABOUT YOU, ALL THE TIME, I SEE YOU EVERYWHERE
BUT I'M TRYING TO, GET OVER YOU, AND OUR OLD LOVE AFFAIR

LAST NIGHT I WENT OUT ON THE TOWN, TO TRY AND EASE THE PAIN
IT DOESN'T MATTER WHERE I GO, I ALWAYS FEEL THE SAME
I THINK ABOUT YOU ALL THE TIME, IT'S MORE THAN I CAN BARE
BUT I'M TRYING TO, GET OVER YOU, AND OUR OLD LOVE AFFAIR

CHORUS:

> I DRINK AND TRY TO HAVE SOME FUN, AND PASS THE TIME AWAY
> I TRY MY BEST TO FORGET, EACH AND EVERY DAY
> THERE'S JUST NO WAY TO FOOL MY FRIENDS, THEY KNOW I STILL CARE
> I'M STILL TRYING TO, GET OVER YOU, AND OUR OLD LOVE AFFAIR

INSTRUMENTAL:

REPEAT CHORUS:

LOOK AT WHAT LONELY CAN DO

CHORUS:

 JUST LOOK AT WHAT LONELY CAN DO
 IT'S MADE A DIFFERENT WOMAN OF YOU
 IN JUST A SHORT WHILE, YOU FORGOT HOW TO SMILE
 JUST LOOK AT WHAT LONELY CAN DO

HE NEVER CARED, THAT YOU GAVE ALL YOU HAD
YOU KNOW WHAT IT MEANS, TO BE LONELY AND SAD
HE TOOK ALL YOUR LOVE, BROKE YOUR HEART INTO
NOW AIN'T IT A SHAME, WHAT LONELY CAN DO

REPEAT CHORUS:

INSTRUMENTAL:

YOU CHOSE THE WRONG ONE, TO GIVE YOUR LOVE TO
HE DOESN'T CARE, WHAT HE PUT YOU THROUGH
HE PLAYED WITH YOUR MIND, NOW IT'S TELLING ON YOU
LORD AIN'T IT A SHAME, WHAT LONELY CAN DO

REPEAT CHORUS:

PUT IT OFF TILL LATER LIES

WHEN YOU TOLD ME YOU WOULD CALL
MADE ME FILL SO GOOD INSIDE
I REALLY LOVED YOU AFTER ALL
ENOUGH TO PUT AWAY MY PRIDE

I NEVER WANTED US TO PART
BUT I COULD SEE SO VERY WELL
YOU WOULD ONLY BREAK MY HEART
AND RIGHT AWAY YOU'D START TO TELL

CHORUS:
    ANOTHER PUT IT OFF TILL LATER LIE
    FULL OF KISSES FILLED WITH BRIBES
    I SEE RIGHT THROUGH THEM EVERY TIME
    THOSE PUT IT OFF TILL LATER LIE'S

DARLING JUST WHAT DID I DO
DOSE IT EVER BOTHER YOU
THE WAY YOU MADE ME FEEL SO BLUE
ALL THE THINGS YOU'VE PUT ME THROUGH

WELL OK I'LL LET YOU GO
FREEDOM BELLS NOW YOU CAN SEE
I JUST WANTED YOU TO KNOW
THERE'S NO NEED FOR YOU TELLING ME

REPEAT CHORUS:

THIS OLE BOY JUST DON'T CARE

I GOT MY CLOTHES DOWN AT THE SALVATION ARMY
I EAT MY MEALS DOWN AT THE HAMBURGER STAND
SOMETIMES I'VE GOT A QUARTER FOR THE JUKEBOX
AND THE IRS DON'T KNOW WHO I AM

I DON'T OWN A BIG HOUSE IN THE COUNTRY
DON'T HAVE A FANCY CAR, TO DRIVE AROUND
I DON'T HAVE THE WORRY, OR THE BIG BILLS
THAT KINDA STUFF ALWAYS GOT ME DOWN

CHORUS:

> I GOT OUT OF THE RAT RACE, WORKING ALL THE TIME
> THEN PAY IT ALL IN TAXES RIGHT DOWN TO MY LAST DIME
> THOSE FLEES CAN FIND ANOTHER DOG THAT THEY FEED UPON
> THIS OLE BOYS BEEN RODE TO HARD TO LONG

BRIDGE:

NOW I DON'T PAY NO FOREIGN AID, OR SOMEONE ELSE RENT
AND UNLIKE WHEN I USE TO WORK, I'VE STILL GOT FIFTEEN CENTS
BROKE TIRED AND HUNGRY, THAT'S HOW I USE TO BE
BUT THEN I DISCOVERED, I DIDN'T HAVE TO BE ALL THREE

REPEAT CHORUS:

THORNS IN MY HEART

MY HEART HAS BEEN BROKEN, AND IT MENDED IN TIME
I'VE HAD TEARDROPS A PLENTY, NOW THERE HARD TO FIND
I'VE KNOWN THE SADNESS OF BEING APART
BUT THERE'S NOTHING AS BAD, AS THESE THORNS IN MY HEART

I'VE KNOWN THE SUFFERING, THE HEARTACHE AND PAIN
WHEN THE ONE THAT YOU CARE FOR, IS PLAYING A GAME
AND YOU FIND, YOU'VE BEEN PLAYING THE LOOSING PART
BUT THERE'S NOTHING AS BAD, AS THESE THORNS IN MY HEART

CHORUS:

    YOU LEFT THORNS IN MY HEART THAT I CAN'T OVERCOME
    YOU TOOK ALL MY LOVE AND THEN LEFT ME WITH NONE
    THEY SAY THAT ALL HEARTACHES PASS, GIVEN TIME
    BUT YOU LEFT BIG OLD THORNS, IN THIS POOR HEART OF MINE

MY HEART IT WON'T EVER, BE QUITE THE SAME
AND ALL THINGS THAT TOUCH IT, CAUSES SUCH PAIN
AND THE HURT KEEPS ON GROWING, EACH TIME I START
TO PULL OUT THESE THORNS, THAT YOU'VE LEFT IN MY HEART

REPEAT CHORUS:

WAKE UP WAKE UP! OH! SINFUL MAN

THE WORLD CALLS FOR BARRABUS
BUT THE SON THEY CANNOT SEE
WHEN CAME THE PERFECT SON OF GOD
THEY NAILED HIM TO A TREE
THEY STILL PREFER THE DARKNESS
THO THE LIGHT SHINES BRIGHT ALL DAY
THEY CLOSE THERE EYES TO JESUS
AND SAY, "TAKE HIM AWAY"

CHORUS:

WAKE UP, WAKE UP, OH! SINFUL MAN
YOU CAN'T SAVE YOURSELF, BUT I KNOW JESUS CAN
THE SON OF GOD PAID THE PRICE
THAT WE MIGHT HAVE ETERNAL LIFE
WAKE UP, WAKE UP, OH! SINFUL MAN

WHEN COMES THE JUDGEMENT MORNING
ALL THINGS WILL BE REVEALED
THEY HAVE NO COVER FOR THERE SINS
THEIR FINAL DOOM IS SEALED
IT WOULD HAVE BEEN SO SIMPLE
THE GIFT FROM GOD IS FREE
THEN YOU WOULD HAVE HAD, THE GIFT OF LIFE
THROUGH OUT ETERNITY

REPEAT CHORUS:

WASHED IN TEARS

THERE'S SOME FLOWERS ON THE TABLE
HE HAD SENT HER LAST WEEK
THE CARD THAT CAME WITH THEM
CHOKES HER SO SHE CAN'T SPEAK
HIS PICTURES ON THE WALL
HE SEEMS SO MUCH ALIVE
TODAY SHE IS HIS WIDOW
YESTERDAY SHE WAS HIS WIFE

CHORUS:

LIFE CAN BE OVER WAY TO SOON
A COOL DREARY MORNING
OR WHEN THE ROSES BLOOM
LET PEOPLE KNOW YOU LOVE THEM
HAVE NO HATE IN YOUR HEART
YOU NEVER KNOW THE INSTANT
THAT YOUR LIFE WILL DEPART

SHE KNOWS THAT HE'S IN HEAVEN
AND IN AN ANGEL BAND
LOVED ONES ARE WITH HIS BODY
AS IT DROPS BENEATH THE SAND
FRIENDS WATCHING FROM HIS GRAVESIDE
AND HE'S WATCHING FROM ABOVE
NOW HE'S A HOLY SPIRIT
HE'S BEEN BATHED IN GOD'S LOVE

LIKE SAND FROM AN HOUR GLASS
OUR LIFE JUST SLIPS AWAY
YOU DON'T KNOW HOW MUCH IS LEFT
OR HOW LONG YOU CAN STAY

SO DO GOOD TO YOUR NEIGHBOR
AS YOU JOURNEY ON YOUR WAY
FOR THE LORD MIGHT SMILE DOWN ON YOU
AND TAKE YOU HOME TODAY

REPEAT CHORUS:

BLACK COAL MINE, WHITE MOONSHINE

WAY BACK IN THE MOUNTAINS, KENTUCKY SURE IS FINE
MY DADDY WORKED IN THE BLACK COAL MINE
BUT I MADE WHITE MOONSHINE

GO TO WORK LIKE ME SON A GOOD JOB IS HARD TO FIND
I CAN GET YOU ON IN THE BLACK COAL MINE
DON'T MAKE THAT WHITE MOONSHINE

CHORUS:

> AND EVERY TIME HE TOLD ME
> YOU'RE BOUND TO GET CAUGHT SOMETIME
> THEY'LL LOCK YOU IN PRISON BOY
> FOR MAKING WHITE MOONSHINE

INSTRUMENTAL BREAK:

SEARCHING MY PAST I WONDER, JUST WHERE I WENT ASTRAY
I LOVED MY DEAR OLD DADDY
BUT WE NEITHER ONE KNEW THE RIGHT WAY

CHORUS:

> HOW MY MEMORIES LINGER
> TEN YEARS I'M DOING TIME
> DADDY WAS KILLED IN THE BLACK COAL MINE
> AND I WAS CAUGHT MAKING WHITE MOONSHINE

DON'T PLAY THAT SONG AGAIN

CHORUS:

> DON'T PLAY THAT SONG AGAIN, WHERE HE'S ALONE AGAIN
> WITH A HURT THAT JUST WON'T END, TO BLUE TO CRY
> DON'T PLAY THAT SONG AGAIN, I'M BEGGING YOU MY FRIEND
> I'LL START REMEMBERING WHEN, SHE SAID GOODBYE

I DON'T UNDERSTAND, WHY SHE HAD TO GO
BUT I STILL HAVE THESE MEMORIES, OF SOMEONE I LOVED SO
I KNOW THAT IT'S NOT OVER, SO WHY SHOULD I PRETEND
I'LL HEAR ANOTHER SAD SONG, AND I'LL JUST HURT AGAIN

REPEAT CHORUS:

I'VE GOT ALL THE PIECES, OF MY BROKEN HEART
I'D PUT THEM BACK TOGETHER, IF I KNEW WHERE TO START
SHOULD I KEEP ON HOPING, THAT SHE'LL COME BACK TO ME
OR FIND A WAY TO MEND THIS HEART, AND LOOSE THESE MEMORIES

REPEAT CHORUS:

ETERNALLY YOURS

WE RAISED A FAMILY TOGETHER, OUR HOUSE WAS A HOME
WE HAD GOOD AND BAD TIMES, SOMETHINGS I DID ALL WRONG
BUT I TRULY LOVED YOU, THO I DIDN'T TELL YOU SO
I JUST THOUGHT DEEP IN YOUR HEART, SURELY YOU WOULD KNOW

CHORUS:

> ETERNALLY YOURS, IF YOU WOULD JUST LOVE ME
> ETERNALLY YOURS, BUT I CAN'T MAKE YOU SEE
> THE PROBLEMS OF LIFE, WE'LL FACE THEM TOGETHER
> WITH GOD BY OUR SIDE, I'M ETERNALLY YOURS

OUR CHILDREN ARE GROWN, AND I HOPE THERE HAPPY
I KNOW THINGS COULD BE BETTER, IF WE WERE STILL ONE
BUT IT'S SO VERY HARD, TO PUT THINGS TOGETHER
OUR PAST IS BEHIND US, AND IT'S OVER AND DONE

REPEAT CHORUS:

FALLING APART AT THE DREAMS

MY MAMA SHE ONCE TOLD ME A STITCH IN TIME SAVES NINE
SHE'D ALWAYS MEND MY OLD BLUE JEANS, JUST IN THE NICK OF TIME
THE SAME HOLDS TRUE FOR LOVERS, PATCH UP THE SLIGHTEST TEAR
WITH LOTS OF HUGS AND KISSES, LET THEM KNOW YOU REALLY CARE

ADVICE I DIDN'T HOLD TO, I LET IT SLIP AWAY
NOW I KNOW, I SHOULD HAVE TOLD HER, EVERY SINGLE DAY
I DIDN'T LET HER, KNOW ABOUT, ALL MY HOPES AND DREAMS
SHOULD HAVE HAD HER UNDERSTAND, NOW WE'VE LOST OUR LOVE IT
     SEEMS

CHORUS:

     NOW I'M, FALLING APART AT THE DREAMS
     LOVE IS NOT AS EASY, AS IT SEEMS
     I CAN'T GET BY WITHOUT HER, IS REALLY WHAT I MEAN
     NOW I'M, FALLING APART AT THE DREAMS

WE HELD ON TO EACH OTHER, WE NEVER WERE APART
I WAS SO IN LOVE WITH YOU, AND YOU WERE IN MY HEART
I THOUGHT SOMEDAY WE'D MARRY, AND I'D CARRY YOU AWAY
TO A CASTLE ON A MOUNTAIN TOP, AND RAISE A FAMILY

REPEAT CHORUS:

FIND OUT WHAT'S RIGHT OR WRONG

FIND OUT WHAT'S RIGHT OR WRONG, BEFORE YOU PUT IT IN THE WORDS
OF A SONG
DON'T YOU BE RESPONSIBLE FOR TELLING SOMEBODY WRONG
YOU MIGHT BE THE ONE TO CAUSE SOMEONE TO GO ASTRAY
AND YOU'LL BE HELD ACCOUNTABLE FOR IT ALL ON JUDGMENT DAY

NOW LISTEN ALL YOU WRITERS, TO WHAT I HAVE TO SAY
DON'T MAKE THEM FOLKS YOUR WRITING TO, THINK THAT IT'S OK
TO CHEAT AND STEAL AND SAY FOR REAL, THINGS THAT JUST AIN'T SO
THESE THINGS WILL ALL BE WRITTEN DOWN, AND SOMEDAY ALL WILL
KNOW

FIND OUT WHAT'S RIGHT OR WRONG, BEFORE YOU PUT IT IN THE WORDS
OF A SONG
DON'T YOU BE RESPONSIBLE FOR TELLING SOMEBODY WRONG
YOU MIGHT BE THE ONE TO CAUSE SOMEONE TO GO ASTRAY
AND YOU'LL BE HELD ACCOUNTABLE FOR IT ALL ON JUDGMENT DAY

I'M NOT AFRAID TO WRITE A SONG ABOUT SOME LOW DOWN THINGS
BUT DON'T GLORIFY AND TRY TO HIDE, THE MISERY THAT IT BRINGS
TELL THE TRUTH, YEA TELL IT STRAIGHT DESTRUCTION IS THAT WAY
FORGIVEN BY THE LOVE OF GOD, EVERY THINGS GONNA BE OK

FIND OUT WHAT'S RIGHT OR WRONG, BEFORE YOU PUT IT IN THE WORDS
OF A SONG
DON'T YOU BE RESPONSIBLE FOR TELLING SOMEBODY WRONG
YOU MIGHT BE THE ONE TO CAUSE, SOMEONE TO GO ASTRAY
AND YOU'LL BE HELD ACCOUNTABLE FOR IT ALL ON JUDGMENT DAY

I DON'T CARE, I DO

YOU KNOW THAT LITTLE OLE WIFE OF MINE
SHE CALLED ME A SILLY WRETCH
SHE SAID WHY DON'T YOU WRITE A HIT SONG
GO TO NASHVILLE AND STRIKE IT RICH
BUY ME ALL THEM THINGS I NEED
LIKE A BRAND NEW CADILLAC OR TWO
YOU SEE SHE DON'T LIKE MY MUSIC
BUT I DON'T CARE, I DO

INSTRUMENTAL BREAK:

ME AND OLD DOC MARTIN
THAT'S MY GUITAR'S NAME
WHY WE SIT AND PICK, FOR MANY AN HOUR
AND LISTEN TO HER COMPLAIN
SHE SAYS YOU CALL THAT RACKET MUSIC
WELL IF ANY LIKE IT IT'S JUST A FEW
YOU SEE SHE DON'T LIKE MY MUSIC
BUT I DON'T CARE, I DO

INSTRUMENTAL BREAK:

NOW ME AND OLD DOC, GIVE IT ALL WE'VE GOT
AND ALL WE GET'S ABUSE
TRYING TO FIND A SONG SHE'LL LIKE
BUT I GUESS IT JUST AIN'T NO USE
WE'VE BEEN BOOED AT BY A PLENTY
AND CHEERED BY ONLY A FEW
YOU SEE THEY DON'T LIKE MY MUSIC
BUT I DON'T CARE, I DO

LIFE'S ADVENTURE – FROM THEN TILL WHEN

INSTRUMENTAL BREAK:

WELL I TOOK MY SONGS TO NASHVILLE
THEY SAID BOY YOU MUST BE KIDDING
WHY IF YOU'VE GOT ANY TALENT AT ALL
I'LL GUARANTEE YOU, IT'S WELL HIDDEN
NOW WHY DON'T YOU JUST GET ON BACK HOME
AND IT'D BE BEST IF YOU FLEW
SEE THEY DIDN'T LIKE MY MUSIC EITHER
BUT I DON'T CARE, I DO

IF IT DOESN'T RAIN

THE LETTERS THAT HE WROTE TO HER, FILLED HER TENDER HEART
THEY TOLD OF THINGS THAT HE'D ENDURE, SO THEY WOULD NEVER BE
    APART
HIS WORDS TOUCHED HER DEEP INSIDE, SHE WOULD SURELY BE HIS BRIDE
UNTIL SHE READ THEM A FEW MORE TIMES, THEN BEGIN TO ANALYZE

HE SAID I'D SWIM A RAGING RIVER, FILLED WITH CROCODILES
CRAWL THROUGH A SNAKE INFESTED JUNGLE, JUST TO SIT WITH YOU A
    WHILE
I LOVE YOU SO MUCH DARLING, I'M ABOUT TO GO INSANE
AND I'LL SEE YOU IN CHURCH NEXT SUNDAY, IF IT DOESN'T RAIN

CHORUS:

    I'LL SEE YOU NEXT SUNDAY, IF IT DOESN'T RAIN
    TOOK AWAY ALL THE FOG, AND LET HER SEE SO PLAIN
    THIS ROMEO IS GOOD WITH WORDS
    BUT A LITTLE SHORT ON BRAINS
    SHE'S STILL CLINGING TO THAT LINE, IF IT DOESN'T RAIN

HE SAID I'D CRAWL A RAT INFESTED GUTTER, DRINK HABENYERO STRAIGHT
FIGHT A RAGING BULL, BEAR HANDED, AND SERVE HIM ON A PLATE
I LOVE YOU THIS MUCH DARLING, SO I'LL MAKE VERY PLAIN
I'LL SEE YOU THIS WEEK END, IF IT DOESN'T RAIN

REPEAT CHORUS:

I'M STILL ALL ALONE AND MISSING YOU

THE BLOOMS OF SPRING, HAVE COME AND GONE
IT'S A LOVELY TIME, BUT I'M ALL ALONE
YOUR BUSY SCHEDULES KEEPING YOU AWAY
YOU SAY YOU'D RATHER BE HERE TO
BUT WITH YOUR JOB THERE'S JUST SO MUCH TO DO
AND I'M STILL ALL ALONE, AND MISSING YOU

IT'S SUMMER NOW THE SUN IS HOT
I WORKED OUR LITTLE GARDEN SPOT
WHY YOU SHOULD SEE THE TOMATO THAT I GREW
BLUEBERRIES, GRAPES AND I HOPE THEY'LL BE
APPLES HANGING ON OUR TREE
BUT I'M STILL ALL ALONE, AND MISSING YOU

CHORUS:

> I THANK THE LORD, HE'S GIVEN ME
> SO MANY LOVELY THINGS TO SEE
> BUT WITHOUT SOMEONE TO SHARE IT HERE WITH ME
> I HOPE THE LORD WILL MAKE YOU SEE
> JUST HOW MUCH YOU MEAN TO ME
> AND I'M STILL ALL ALONE, AND MISSING YOU

INSTRUMENTAL BREAK:

REPEAT CHORUS:

TAG:

> YES I'M STILL ALL ALONE AND MISSING YOU

LOVE GONE RIGHT

EVERYONE IS SINGING, A SAD COUNTRY SONG
AND EVERY SONG IS TELLING, ABOUT THAT A LOVE THAT'S GONE WRONG
TEARDROPS AND HEARTACHES ARE NO PART OF ME TONIGHT
DON'T WANT TO SING ABOUT ANYTHING, BUT A LOVE THAT'S GONE RIGHT

CHORUS:

    I'VE GOT A LOVE THAT'S GONE RIGHT FOR ME
    I'M HAPPY NOW AS I COULD BE
    MAKES ME WANT TO STAY HOME EVERY NIGHT
    I DON'T KNOW WHAT SHE SEES IN ME
    BUT I NEVER WANT TO BE SET FREE
    I KNOW FOR SURE, THAT SHE LOVES ME
    I'VE GOT A LOVE THAT'S GONE RIGHT

EVERYBODY KNOWS THE TUNE, OF A SAD COUNTRY SONG
AND EVERYONE'S HEARD ALL ABOUT A LOVE THAT'S GONE WRONG
BUT OUR KIND OF TRUE LOVE, IS REALLY OUT OF SIGHT
DON'T WANT TO SING ABOUT ANYTHING, BUT A LOVE THAT'S GONE RIGHT

I PRAY FOR SAD SONG WRITERS THAT SOMEDAY THEY MAY FEEL
ALL THE JOY AND HAPPINESS, OF TRUE LOVE WHEN IT'S REAL
WHEN THEY DO, THEY'LL TAKE OFF LIKE A HUMMINGBIRD IN FLIGHT
GRAB A PEN AND WRITE AGAIN, ABOUT A LOVE THAT'S GONE RIGHT

REPEAT CHORUS:

MY LOVE FOR YOU IS GONE

MORE THAN A YEAR AGO, YOU BROKE MY HEART IN TWO
THAT WAS WHEN YOU TOLD ME, THAT YOU'D FOUND SOMEONE NEW
NOW YOU COME BACK TO ME, WANTING OUR LOVE TO GO ON
I'VE BEEN ALONE, FOR SO LONG, MY LOVE FOR YOU IS GONE

YOU SAY YOU NEVER CARED FOR HIM, YOU JUST DID IT FOR SPITE
BUT THAT BROKE UP A PART OF ME, THAT TRIED TO DO WHAT'S RIGHT
NOW LOVE HAS GONE ANOTHER ROAD, I MUST GO ON ALONE
I'VE BEEN ALONE FOR SO LONG, MY LOVE FOR YOU IS GONE

INSTRUMENTAL BREAK:

SO LONG, AND MAY GOD BLESS YOU, AND I'LL SHOW YOU THE DOOR
I HOPE YOU FIND WITH ALL MY HEART WHAT YOU'VE BEEN SEARCHING FOR
BUT YOU LIVE IN ANOTHER WORLD, I MUST GO ON ALONE
I'VE BEEN ALONE, FOR SO LONG, MY LOVE FOR YOU IS GONE

TAG:

I'VE BEEN ALONE, FOR SO LONG, MY LOVE FOR YOU IS GONE

NEVER AGAIN

FOR MANY YEARS, I'VE LOVED YOU LADY
AND WE HAVE DANCED, IN MANY ROOMS
NOW THAT OUR BODY'S HAVE AGED
IT'S HARD TO FIND, A NIMBLE TUNE
SO TONIGHT, JUST HOLD ME CLOSELY
THINK HOW GOOD, IT HAS BEEN
AND PLEASE DON'T LET FOREVER
TURN INTO, NEVER AGAIN

NOW I KNOW THAT, YOUTH IS FLEETING
BUT MY HEART, STILL HOLDS, YOU TRUE
A GREAT LIFE SPENT TOGETHER
NOW THERE'S SOME THINGS WE CAN'T DO
BUT I'LL ALWAYS REMEMBER
JUST HOW GOOD, IT HAS BEEN
PLEASE DON'T LET FOREVER
TURN INTO, NEVER AGAIN

CHORUS:

WHEN YOUR LIFE IS ANCHORED
YOU KNOW GOD, HAS MADE A WAY
THERE'S A MANSON, WAITING FOR YOU
THERE'S JUST ONE THING, YOU CAN SAY
THANK YOU LORD, FOR YOUR MERCY
AND PAYING FOR, ALL MY SINS
I KNOW THAT FOREVER
WON'T TURN INTO, NEVER AGAIN

PRAISE THE LORD AND SHOUT

NOW THE WICKED MAN HE DENIES, GOD'S RECORD OF HIS SON
CAN'T BELIEVE HE'LL STAND IN JUDGMENT, WHEN LIFE ON EARTH IS DONE
THE BIBLE TELLS, THE PIT OF HELL'S, FOR THE DEVIL AND HIS KIND
BUT HE CAN'T STEAL MY HEART AWAY, THE LORDS DONE PAID FOR MINE

CHORUS:

YOU CAN GET SALVATION, IT'S EASY AND IT'S FREE
PAID FOR BY JESUS, FOR US ON CALVARY
I TELL YOU IT'S A GIFT OF GOD, AND YOU CAN'T WORK IT OUT
NO NEED TO TRY AND PAY FOR IT
JUST PRAISE THE LORD AND SHOUT

THE WICKED MAN SAYS, SHOW ME, AND THEN I MIGHT BELIEVE
THINKS HE'S TO SMART, WITHIN HIS HEART, CAN'T BE THAT NAIVE
BUT JESUS SAID, IF YOU BELIEVE, I'LL TELL YOU WHAT I'LL DO
I'LL SEND THE HOLY SPIRIT DOWN, AND HE'LL SHOW IT ALL TO YOU

REPEAT CHORUS:

SECRET HIDEAWAY

WHEN I PICKED YOU UP THIS MORNING
WE'D PLANNED, THE PERFECT HOLIDAY
WE'D HAVE A PICNIC IN THE MOUNTAINS
AND GO TO OUR, SECRET HIDEAWAY
IT WAS, A SPECIAL, OUTING
AND I'D, JUST LIKE, TO SAY
THERE'S NOTHING ELSE, IN THIS WORLD
LIKE OUR SECRET, HIDEAWAY

CHORUS:
 WHEN WE WERE KIDS, WE SPENT OUR TIME THERE

    PLAYING IN THE SAND
    LONG BEFORE, WE GREW UP
    TO BE, A WOMAN AND A MAN
    BUT, WE LIKE, TO GO THERE STILL
    AND SOMETIMES, SPEND THE DAY
    PLAYING IN THE SAND, AT OUR OLD HIDEAWAY

NOW THAT WE, HAVE GROWN, MUCH OLDER
REMEMBER, HOW WE USED, TO PLAY
I WISH THAT WE, COULD GO BACK AGAIN
TO OUR, SECRET HIDEAWAY
THANK GOD, FOR MY MEMORIES
AND FOR GUIDING ME, EACH DAY
AND FOR SENDING, ME, A GIRL LIKE YOU
AND A SECRET HIDEAWAY

INSTRUMENTAL BREAK:

REPEAT CHORUS:

THE LOVE OF JESUS

IT WAS EARLY IN MY CHILDHOOD
WHEN I WENT TO SUNDAY SCHOOL
THAT I LEARNED ALL ABOUT
THE LOVE OF JESUS

AND AS I GREW OLDER
WHERE THEY TAUGHT THE GOLDEN RULE
THAT I LEARNED MORE ABOUT
THE LOVE OF JESUS

CHORUS:

> THE LOVE OF JESUS
> IS SO WONDERFUL TO ME
> THE ONLY WAY TO HEAVEN
> IT'S HIS LOVE THAT SETS US FREE
> SO OPEN UP YOUR HEART
> HE'S SOMEONE YOU CAN TRUST
> AND LEARN MORE ABOUT
> THE LOVE OF JESUS

INSTRUMENTAL BREAK:

MANY YEARS HAVE GONE BY
STILL EVERY DAY I TRY
TO LEARN MORE ABOUT
THE LOVE OF JESUS

TO SAVE YOUR SOUL FROM SIN
THE ONE WAY YOU CAN WIN
IS TO LEARN MORE ABOUT
THE LOVE OF JESUS

REPEAT CHORUS:

SILENT MEMORIES

SILENTLY YOUR MEMORY COMES WALKING THRU MY MIND
AND CAREFULLY I TRY TO HIDE, THE TEARDROPS IN MY EYES
IT TEARS APART MY BROKEN HEART AS THOUGHTS OF YOU ENTWINE
ABOUT YOUR SILENT MEMORY WALKING THRU MY MIND

SILENTLY YOUR MEMORY COMES WALKING THRU MY MIND
CONSTANTLY IT TORTURES ME I CAN'T LEAVE IT BEHIND
WHEN DREAMS APPEAR YOU'RE ALWAYS NEAR AND I CAN'T SEEM TO FIND
A THING TO KEEP YOUR MEMORY FROM WALKING THRU MY MIND

CHORUS:

    YES YOUR MEMORY COMES WALKING
    WALKING THRU MY MIND
    THEY ALWAYS CAUSE THESE TEARDROPS
    TEARS THAT I CAN'T HIDE
    IT TEARS APART MY BROKEN HEART
    MY LOVE FOR YOU WAS BLIND
    SILENTLY YOUR MEMORY
    COMES WALKING THRU MY MIND

INSTRUMENTAL BREAK:

REPEAT CHORUS:

WHERE WERE YOU

WHERE WERE YOU WHEN ALL MY DREAMS WERE SHATTERED
WHERE WERE YOU WHEN MY HEART WAS BROKEN IN TWO
WITH NO HOPE TO CLING TO WITHOUT SOMEONE TO HOLD ME
WHEN I WAS OH SO LONESOME DARLING WHERE WERE YOU

WHERE WERE YOU WHEN SHE SAID SHE'D FOUND ANOTHER
WHERE WERE YOU WHEN SHE LEFT WITH THAT SOMEBODY NEW
WHEN I WAS OH SO LONESOME DROWNING IN MY SORROW
WHEN I WAS FREE TO LOVE YOU DARLING WHERE WERE YOU

CHORUS:

>   NOW I'M MARRIED TO ANOTHER
>   ALTHO TRUE LOVE I'VE NEVER FOUND
>   SHE PICKED ME UP WHEN I WAS A LONG WAY DOWN
>   AND DARLING NOW I'VE FOUND YOU
>   AND YOU THRILL ME THRU AND THRU
>   WHEN I WAS FREE TO LOVE DARLING
>   WHERE WERE YOU

INSTRUMENTAL BREAK:

WHERE WERE YOU WHEN THEM BIG OLD TEARDROPS WERE FALLING
WHERE WERE YOU WHEN I WAS NEEDING SOMEBODY NEW
WHEN I WAS OH SO LONESOME DROWNING IN MY SORROW
WHEN I WAS FREE TO LOVE YOU DARLING
WHERE WERE YOU

TAG:

>   WHEN I WAS FREE TO LOVE YOU DARLING
>   WHERE WERE YOU

I'D BE SATISFIED

I AM NEVER, NEVER HAPPY AND I WONDER WHY I'M NOT
I'M FOREVER WISHING FOR THINGS THAT I AIN'T GOT
I'M ALWAYS FILLED WITH ENVY WHEN I SEE A WEALTHY MAN
WHY CAN'T I BE WEALTHY TOO WHEN I DO THE BEST I CAN

CHORUS:

    IF I COULD BE WHERE I AIN'T, DO WHAT I CAN'T
    AND HAVE WHAT I AIN'T GOT, THEN I'D BE SATISFIED

I'VE TRAVELED ROUND THIS COUNTRY YES I'VE BEEN MOST EVERYWHERE
EACH TIME I STOP TO SETTLE DOWN, I FIND I DON'T LIKE IT THERE
I HAVE NO PLACE TO CALL HOME LIKE OTHER FRIENDS I KNOW
AND HARD LUCK SEEMS TO FOLLOW ME EVERY WHERE I GO

REPEAT CHORUS:

INSTRUMENTAL BREAK:

I HEAR A TRAIN A COMING LISTEN TO THE WHISTLE BLOW
FARE YE WELL GOOD PEOPLE IT'S TIME FOR ME TO GO
IF THERE'S AN EMPTY BOXCAR THEN THAT'S WHERE I WILL RIDE
AND IF THAT TRAIN DON'T EVER STOP THEN I'LL BE SATISFIED

REPEAT CHORUS:

HOW CAN SOMETHING SO RIGHT
BE SO WRONG

I LIE HERE IN BED WITH MY RADIO ON
AND TRY NOT TO THINK ABOUT YOU
BUT YOUR MEMORY WALTZES RIGHT INTO MY MIND
AND I'M LONESOME THE WHOLE NIGHT THROUGH

CHORUS:

SO HOLD ME WHILE WE HAVE THE TIME
I KNOW IT CAN'T LAST VERY LONG
AND KISS ME GOODBYE WHEN YOU GO
HOW CAN SOMETHING SO RIGHT BE SO WRONG

EACH TIME YOU LEAVE ME I TRY NOT TO CRY
BUT INSIDE I'M SURE FEELING BLUE
AND IT BRAKES MY HEART WHEN YOU WALK OUT THE DOOR
CAUSE SOMEONE'S HOME WAITING FOR YOU

REPEAT CHORUS:

SO HOLD ME WHILE WE HAVE THE TIME
I KNOW IT CAN'T LAST VERY LONG
AND KISS ME GOODBYE WHEN YOU GO
HOW CAN SOMETHING SO RIGHT BE SO WRONG

DRINKING SEEMS RIGHT

SOMETIMES I DO TO MUCH DRINKING
WHEN I ONLY WANT TO HOLD YOU TIGHT
AND THEN I REMEMBER HOW YOU HURT ME ON THAT NIGHT
THAT MAKES DRINKING ALMOST SEEM ALRIGHT
THAT MAKES DRINKING ALMOST SEEM ALRIGHT

SOMETIMES I GET THAT LOW DOWN FEELING
BUT IT ONLY HAUNTS ME DAY AND NIGHT
YOU CAUSED THE PAIN BROUGHT ME SHAME JUST DIDN'T DO ME RIGHT
AND THAT MAKES DRINKING ALMOST SEEM ALRIGHT
THAT MAKES DRINKING ALMOST SEEM ALRIGHT

CHORUS:

> SOMEDAY I KNOW, I'LL DROWN MY SORROW
> AND FACE UP TO WHAT I KNOW IS TRUE
> I FEEL SUCH PAIN, WHEN I HEAR YOUR NAME
> I GET THESE LOW DOWN BLUES
> THAT MAKES DRINKING ALMOST SEEM ALRIGHT
> THAT MAKES DRINKING ALMOST SEEM ALRIGHT

INSTRUMENTAL BREAK:

REPEAT CHORUS:

GEORGIA WOMAN

GEORGIA WOMAN THAT TOUCH OF SADNESS
IN YOUR CRYING WON'T CHANGE MY MIND
ALTHO I WANT TO WE CAN'T UNDO
THE PAIN YOU CAUSED ME IS TO MUCH THIS TIME

CHORUS:

    I'M NOT GONNA LET YOU MAKE A FOOL OUT OF ME
    THE WAY THINGS HAVE BEEN SO LONG
    THEY'RE JUST NOT GONNA BE
    YOU'VE TAUGHT ME WELL IN YOUR SCHOOL
    OF HURT AND MISERY
    MOST OF ALL I LEARNED YOU DON'T LOVE ME

INSTRUMENTAL BREAK:

GEORGIA WOMAN I AIN'T DENYING
YOU HAVE SURE HAD A HOLD ON MY MIND
ONE THING I CAN'T DO RIGHT NOW IS HOLD YOU
THE GAME IS OVER IT WON'T WORK THIS TIME

CHORUS:

    I'M NOT GONNA LET YOU MAKE A FOOL OUT OF ME
    THE WAY THINGS HAVE BEEN SO LONG
    THEY'RE JUST NOT GONNA BE
    YOU'VE TAUGHT ME WELL IN YOUR SCHOOL
    OF HURT AND MISERY
    MOST OF ALL I LEARNED YOU DON'T LOVE ME

WHAT SHALL I DO WITH JESUS

PILATE TOLD THE PEOPLE AT THE TIME OF THE FEAST
JESUS OR BARABBAS WHOM DO YOU WANT RELEASED
WHAT SHALL I DO WITH JESUS, THE ONE THEY CALL THE CHRIST
AND THEY ALL SAID TO HIM, LET HIM BE CRUCIFIED

PILATE WAS SO FEARFUL AS HE TOOK HIS STAND
HE CALLED FOR SOME WATER TO WASH THE BLOOD OFF OF HIS HANDS
HIS BLOOD BE UPON US AND OUR CHILDREN THEY CRIED
SO HE GAVE THEM BARABBAS AND THE LORD WAS CRUCIFIED

CHORUS:

HIS BLOOD IS ON OUR HANDS TIL IT'S APPLIED TO OUR HEARTS
IT'S ALL UP TO US NOW HE'S ALREADY DONE HIS PART
EACH TIME WE REJECT HIM WE PUT A SPEAR IN HIS SIDE
WHAT SHALL I DO WITH JESUS WE MUST ALL DECIDE

WE WONDER AT THE PEOPLE WHO CHOSE BARABBAS ON THAT DAY
HOW COULD THEY BE SO FOOLISH AND TURN THE LORD AWAY
THEN WE LEAVE OUR CHURCH AND GO RIGHT BACK TO OUR SIN
JUST LIKE THAT MOB, WE CRUCIFY HIM AGAIN

REPEAT CHORUS:

NO ONE MENDS A BROKEN HEART
LIKE YOU

SOMETIMES I REALLY THINK IT'S OVER
BUT YOUR BLUE EYES HAVE NEVER LOST A FOOL
ONE KISS AND I'M RIGHT BACK WHERE I STARTED
OH! NO ONE MENDS A BROKEN HEART LIKE YOU

YOU ALWAYS SEEM TO FIND THE SCATTERED PIECES
YOUR WORDS TURN LIES BACK INTO TRUTH
PRACTICE MAKES PERFECT DON'T IT DARLING
OH! NO ONE MENDS A BROKEN HEART LIKE YOU

CHORUS:

EACH TIME THAT I GIVE UP, AND I PACK UP TO LEAVE
YOU PUT MAGIC WORDS IN MY EAR, THAT I ALWAYS BELIEVE
I'M HELPLESS AND YOU MAKE ME DO, JUST WHAT YOU WANT ME TO
OH! NO ONE MENDS A BROKEN HEART LIKE YOU

INSTRUMENTAL BREAK:

REPEAT CHORUS:

THE LIES I TOLD TO KEEP YOU

I WASN'T FREE WHEN I MET YOU
BUT I WAS A LONELY MAN
SOME FOLKS MAY THINK YOU CAN'T BE THAT
AND WEAR A WEDDING BAND
BUT MARRIAGE NEVER DID INSURE
LOVE AND, A HAPPY HOME
AND THE LIES I TOLD TO KEEP YOU
ARE THE REASON THAT YOU'RE GONE

IF MY MARRIAGE HAD BEEN KNOWN TO YOU
YOU'D NEVER HAD SPENT THE TIME
IT TAKES TO FALL SO DEEP IN LOVE
SO DEEP THAT LOVE IS BLIND
BUT ONCE YOU FALL THAT DEEP IN LOVE
IT'S HARD TO SEE THE WRONG
AND THE LIES I TOLD TO KEEP YOU
ARE THE REASON THAT YOU'RE GONE

INSTRUMENTAL BREAK:

CHORUS:

> THE LIES I TOLD TO KEEP YOU
> ARE THE REASON THAT YOU'RE GONE
> DARLING HOW CAN THAT BE SO WRONG
> I LOVED YOU OH! SO DEARLY
> I WANTED OUR LOVE TO GO ON
> NOW THE LIES I TOLD TO KEEP YOU
> ARE THE REASON THAT YOU'RE GONE

TAG:

171

YES THE LIES I TOLD TO KEEP YOU
ARE THE REASON THAT YOU'RE GONE

YOU TRIED TO BREAK MY HEART, BUT I ONLY LOST MY MIND

I FELL IN LOVE WITH YOU, AND I TOLD YOU HOW I FEEL
YOU SAID I LOVE YOU TOO, AND I THOUGHT YOUR LOVE WAS REAL
THEN LATER I FOUND OUT YOU WERE THE CHEATING KIND
YOU TRIED TO BREAK MY HEART BUT I ONLY LOST MY MIND

WHEN THE FLAME OF LOVE BURNS DOWN TO JUST A GLOW
AND ONE HEART WANTS THE OTHER, TO LET GO
BUT YOU NEVER TOLD ME AND MY LOVE FOR YOU WAS BLIND
YOU TRIED TO BREAK MY HEART, BUT I ONLY LOST MY MIND

CHORUS:

>   YOU TRIED TO BREAK MY HEART, BUT I ONLY LOST MY MIND
>   IT FELL OFF THE DEEP END, INTO SOME OTHER PLACE AND TIME
>   I GAVE YOU MUCH MORE LOVE, MORE THAN YOU COULD EVER FIND
>   YOU TRIED TO BREAK MY HEART, BUT I ONLY LOST MY MIND

INSTRUMENTAL BREAK:

REPEAT CHORUS:

TAG:

WALKING WITH JESUS

SINCE I'M WALKING WITH JESUS IN THE NEW LOVE THAT I'VE FOUND
MY HEART'S A LITTLE LIGHTER, WITH MY FEET ON SOLID GROUND
I'LL NEVER EVER WALK NO MORE THE WICKED PATH OF SIN
WALKING CLOSE TO JESUS IS THE ONLY WAY TO WIN

CHORUS:

KEEP ME WALKING WITH JESUS
THRU LIFE WITH GOD'S OWN SON
KEEP ME WALKING WITH JESUS
BECAUSE HE'S THE ONLY ONE
KEEP ME WALKING WITH JESUS
I'LL SAY IT ONCE AGAIN
UNTIL I GET TO HEAVEN
THAT'S WHERE IT ALL BEGINS

THE LOVE I LIVE WITH JESUS TURNED MY WHOLE LIFE AROUND
A SONG IS ALWAYS IN MY HEART I LOVE THAT CHRISTIAN SOUND
I DON'T GO AROUND THE PLACES, WHERE I USED TO GO
AND WHY I EVER WENT THERE NOW, I DON'T EVEN KNOW

REPEAT CHORUS:

SONGS I DIDN'T WRITE (BUT WISH I HAD)

The following are some songs that I didn't write, but many of my friends have requested or suggested that I sing.

FOUR WALLS AND A WINDOW
BLUEST HEARTACHE OF THE YEAR
I'M NOT UP TO FEELING DOWN
BUT I LIE
THREE FOR A QUARTER
SILENCE SAYS IT ALL
I'M NOT OVER YOU
SILENT PARTNER
PLAYING POSSUM

Made in the USA
Middletown, DE
07 August 2017